Bath's Luscious Larder

Recipes using ingredients from local food producers

written by Laraine Hare
watercolours by Jan Tozer

Bath's Luscious Larder

Recipes using ingredients from local food producers

First published in the United Kingdom in 2013 by Balmy Kitchen Publishing

ISBN 978-0-9574848-0-1

Recipes by Laraine Hare
Watercolours by Jan Tozer

Photography by Tom Harrison, Leonie Watson and Amanda Goode
Book design by Tom Harrison
Thank you Tom. I could not have done this without you.

Contents
By season, course and food producer

Contents
(continued)

Contents
Producers. products and where to buy

Introduction

I have always loved cooking, so I decided to combine my obsession with food with my love of teaching. I am lucky in having a spacious kitchen in the basement of a Georgian building, so I decided to experiment with my friends, designing cookery sessions, and drinking a great deal of wine in the process! The result was the creation of my cookery school, The Balmy Kitchen: www.balmykittchen.co.uk

I wanted to use as many local and seasonal ingredients as possible, and became inspired by the wonderful people who provide food in the area. This led to two years of research, and the publication of this book, illustrated by my good friend, the watercolour artist, Jan Tozer.

Over the past few years there has been a massive surge in interest in the diversity and quality of British food. We used to be embarrassed by the lack of inspiration in our eating habits, both at home and in restaurants, when compared to those in Italy and France. I believe that our openness to new ideas and our ability to learn from the best cuisines of the world, has led to a glorious expansion of our growing culinary expertise, thanks to the diversity of our home produce.

Rural communities seem to have been re-invigorated by the growth of small producers, who take justifiable pride in both the ethos and quality of their products. Local Agenda 21, a government initiative in the early 1990s, encouraged the production and consumption of local food in order to help deal with some of the social, economic and environmental issues concerning us all. This led to the establishment of the Bath Farmers' Market in 1997, the first in the country.

When visiting Vancouver I was inspired by their love of food in general, and by their '100 mile diet' promoting food produced locally. In response to this, I decided to write this book in appreciation of the farmmers in the area around Bath. We are lucky to be living in a very fertile area, so it is possible to find a great wealth of delicious foods produced within just fifty miles.

Not all of the products I have chosen are organic, but love and dedication are abundantly evident in all of them. I have avoided any that have already been selected for attention by celebrity chefs, and have focused on foods that have not been processed into more complex products such as cakes or breads – delicious as they are!

I apologise to those I have not included. I have simply chosen those who fulfilled my criteria. I am sure there are enough wonderful producers in the area to fill many books!

Spring

Sleight Farm
Goat's cheese producer, Timsbury

Mary Holbrook has been making cheese for over thirty years, and has influenced many cheese makers. She is highly respected among the food producers of the Bath area, as well as having an international reputation. Neal's Yard has been selling her cheeses since the 1980s.

She initially learned her skills in France, but has embraced a range of influences including Portuguese recipes. She is famous for using cardoon stamens in the place of rennet for her Cardo cheese, which makes it popular among vegetarians. When added to the milk it coagulates, forming a curd, which she cuts very gently, using her arms rather than knives or wires, to allow greater sensitivity.

Her farm is on a hilltop outside Timsbury, and she rears free-range British Lop pigs as well as producing her marvellous unpasteurised goat's cheeses. She clearly still loves the whole process of cheese making, and relishes the idiosyncrasies due to seasonal variations, leading to unpredictable elements in her cheeses.

Mary's cheeses:

Cardo:
Goat's cheese made using cardoon (instead of rennet). It is a semi-soft cheese with a washed rind. It has a silky texture, with a gooey centre and a rich, sweet flavour.

Tymsboro:
Mould-ripened goat's cheese. This is a charcoal -coated pyramid shape: dense and creamy, with a lemony flavour and a nutty edge.

Tyning:
A hard sheep's cheese developed from a Sicilian recipe; it is made in a basket mould: dense, smooth and nutty.

Old Ford:
Like an aged Pecorino, or a matured Manchego. Delicious.

Website Address: N/A

Phone Number: N/A

Address:
Timsbury, Near Bath

Opening Times: N/A

Where to Buy:
Bath Farmers' Market
Frome Farmers' Market
Bristol Farmers' Market
Dick Willows, Bathford
Paxton and Whitfield, Bath
Fine Cheese Company, Bath

Where to Eat:
The Glass Boat, Bristol

Goat's Cheese and Puy Lentil Salad
with pancetta and wild garlic

Ingredients:

4 tablespoons Somerset rapeseed oil
2 shallots, chopped
75g pancetta, chopped
3 cloves of garlic, chopped
175g puy lentils
1 bay leaf
1 teaspoon of fresh thyme leaves
600ml stock (without salt)
1 teaspoon wholegrain mustard
1 tablespoon cider vinegar
Some salad leaves
A handful of young wild garlic leaves
200g Cardo goat's cheese, crumbled

Method:

1. Heat 1 tablespoon of the oil in a
   saucepan and fry the shallots until
   golden. Remove from the pan.
2. Fry the pancetta in the same pan, then
   remove and drain on kitchen paper.
3. Fry two cloves of garlic in the same
   pan for a minute. Add the lentils, bay
   leaf and thyme, then add the stock and
   simmer for 25-30 minutes until the
   liquid is absorbed. Season to taste.
4. Make the dressing by crushing the
   remaining garlic with some sea salt in a
   mortar and pestle. Add the mustard,
   then the vinegar. Mix well, then add
   the oil. Season. (Alternatively you can
   make this in a small food processor).
   Pour the dressing over the lentils. Stir.
5. Wash the wild garlic leaves carefully
   then shred them. Place them on a dish
   with the salad leaves and put the lentils
   on top. Sprinkle the shallots, pancetta
   and goat's cheese over the top.

Cardoon Plant (Artichoke Thistle)

13

Eades Market Gardeners
A family greengrocer in Bath

There has been a greengrocer on Crescent Lane since the Second World War. It used to be where St Andrew's School now stands and when it was bombed, people from the neighbourhood came out with orange boxes and bits of furniture to recreate the shop. The family is still very much part of the community, and they feel closely connected to their customers. It feels like a village shop, and Tony knows people whose families have been going there for generations.

The family grows their vegetables on their land on the south-facing slopes of Little Solsbury. The city boundary actually runs through their land, so they couldn't be more local. They grow vegetables in the traditional way, rotating the crops and involving all the family, including their grandchildren, in picking. Skills are passed on from one generation to the next; for example, when they acquire the mechanical skills needed to maintain their tractors, they are said to have 'learnt the spanners'.

Reputation is everything to the family, and this is passed on through word of mouth. They make up to forty deliveries a day, ranging from a small box to half a van full, so it is clear that more and more people are coming to know about the excellent quality on which they can rely. Many restaurants in the area specify on their menus that their vegetables come from Eades, such is their reputation for excellence.

John Hurd's organic watercress:

John Hurd is one of the few people growing organic watercress in this country, and he is the only one who still picks and bunches it by hand. His method is very traditional, with mineral-rich water from underground springs washing away any pests. He has been growing watercress since 1953, but he still loves it, and eats a large bunch of it every day.

He is based in Longbridge Deverill where he cultivates eight acres of watercress all year round. You can order direct from him at www.organicwatercress.co.uk, or you can buy it at Eades greengrocers (see above).

Website Address: N/A

Phone Number:
01225 317319

Address:
18 Crescent Lane, Julian Road,
Bath, BA1 2PX

Opening Times:
Monday - Friday	8.30am - 6pm
Saturday	8.30am - 4pm

Where to Buy:
At their own shop

Where to Eat:
Royal Crescent Hotel, Bath
Demuths Vegetarian Restaurant, Bath
The Olive Tree, Bath
The King William, Bath

Watercress and prosciutto rolls

I have adapted John Hurd's recipe, using local ingredients

Ingredients:

1 tablespoon extra virgin rapeseed oil
2 red onions, finely chopped
1 red pepper, finely chopped
1 clove of garlic, finely chopped
1 chilli, deseeded and finely chopped
2 bunches of watercress, large stems trimmed
8 slices of prosciutto or Parma ham

For the dressing
1 teaspoon mustard
1 tablespoon chives, finely chopped
6 tablespoons extra virgin rapeseed oil
4 tablespoons cider vinegar
1 tablespoon capers

To finish
Shavings of hard cheese such as Old Ford goat's cheese, or Old Demdike sheep's cheese

Method:

1. Fry the onion and red pepper in a little oil until soft, and then add the garlic and chilli.
2. Cook until slightly golden.
3. Add the watercress and cook briefly until just soft. Season with sea salt and freshly ground black pepper.
4. Remove from the heat and place equal quantities on the edge of the ham slices and roll up carefully.
5. Mix the ingredients for the dressing and spoon this over the rolls.
6. Finish with the shavings of your chosen cheese.

Clancy and Sealey
Licensed to sell game in season, Wiltshire

Ted Clancy is a regular stall-holder at Bath Farmers' market, and it is clear that he is passionate about all things related to game. He remembers the old days when game could be sold, complete with feathers or fur, straight from the shoots.

These days, shoots are generally corporate events, and people from all over the world take part. Despite this, there is very little profit in selling game, as it is so expensive to rear the birds. This is because of the cost of insurance and the escalating price of grain. It can cost as much as £18 to rear a pheasant. They sell the birds for about £2 each, so the money made from the shoots is crucial.

There are some small local shoots in the area, which are mainly for the enjoyment of the locals, and are as much about eating and drinking as about the shooting!

Trading standards and public health regulations insist on regular upgrading of premises, which means that many of the old producers have gone out of business. Game must now be packaged and ready to cook; in fact this suits many customers as few people have the time or the skill to prepare the meat themselves.

The 'old times' may have gone, but judging by the interest of the customers at the farmers' market, there is quite a resurgence of interest in game, as it is both free-range and local.

Website Address: N/A

Phone Number:
01747 860121

Address:
21 Castle Hill, Mere,
Wiltshire, BA12 6HL

Opening Times: N/A

Where to Buy:
Bath Farmers' Market

Woodpigeon Breast Roulades
with sage and pesto

Ingredients:

4 boneless woodpigeon breasts
Sea salt
Freshly ground black pepper
8 sage leaves
8 teaspoons pesto
4 slices of finely sliced pancetta
1 tablespoon extra virgin rapeseed oil

Method:

1. Place a woodpigeon breast on a piece of clingfilm, and fold it over to cover the meat. Pound the woodpigeon with a rolling pin to flatten it. Repeat with the rest of the breasts.
2. Season each breast with sea salt and freshly ground black pepper. Place three sage leaves and two teaspoons of pesto on each breast.
3. Roll up the woodpigeon breasts, then wrap each separately in pancetta. You can stretch the pancetta with the flat of a knife to make it longer and thinner.
4. Heat the oil in a pan and fry the roulades, turning until browned all over, for about 30 minutes. Serve with some extra pesto and fresh bread.

Note: you can make your own pesto by simply blending 50g of basil leaves with 20g of parsley leaves, 50 g of pine nuts, 30g of grated Parmesan, a clove of garlic and 50ml of extra virgin rapeseed oil. Season with sea salt and freshly ground black pepper.

Baronet Cheese
The Old Cheese Room, Neston

Julianna Sedli is the only artisan cheese maker in the country to be producing a Reblochon-style cheese from organic, unpasteurised Jersey milk. Everyone I spoke to was very excited about this outstanding cheese, which is the result of much experimentation. Raymond Blanc loved it when he visited Neston Park Farm shop, and it came highly recommended in Paxton and Whitfield.

Julianna is originally from Hungary, where she studied at Agricultural College. She has made cheese in Indiana, where they named a cheese after her, as well as at Neal's Yard and with Mary Holbrook of Sleight Farm. She had been looking for a good source of milk when she discovered the Neston Park Estate, where they have an organic farm with a herd of Jersey cows. She loved the fact that she would be able to make cheese from fresh warm milk straight from the cows on the farm, and that she can sell it in the Neston Park farm shop, just down the road, keeping down the food miles of her product. She works in a calving shed that has been converted for her, surrounded by the fields of lush grass that are crucial for the rich creamy milk produced by the cows.

The cheese is not heat-treated or pressed, but simply ladled into moulds lined with cheesecloth. It is dry-salted to get rid of excess fluid, and then turned regularly as it matures on wooden boards.

Julianna has just produced a new cheese called Wasabi Pearl. It is creamy, with a gentle kick from the wasabi. We are so lucky to have her living in the area, providing us with her delicious cheeses.

Website Address: N/A

Phone Number:
07531 060936

Email Address:
theoldcheeseroom@talktalk.net

Address:
Neston Park Home Farm, Corsham, Wiltshire, SN13 9TG

Opening Times: N/A

Where to Buy:
Neston Park Farm shop, Atworth
Bath Farmers' Market
Dick Willows, Bathford
Paxton and Whitfield, Bath
PJs Farm Stall, Green Park, Bath

Tartiflette

An adaptation of a French recipe that uses Reblochon cheese

Ingredients:

1-2 tablespoons extra virgin rapeseed oil
2 large shallots, sliced
1 large clove of garlic, finely chopped
100g young spinach leaves
1 sweet potato, 350 - 400g
150g Baronet cheese, sliced (including the rind)
50ml double cream
50ml white wine or stock

Method:

1. Heat the oven to 180°c, gas 4.
2. Heat the oil in a large frying pan. Fry the shallots over a medium heat for 5 minutes. Add the garlic and spinach to the pan and cook gently until the spinach has wilted. Season.
3. Peel the sweet potato and slice it finely. Season with sea salt and black pepper.
4. Mix the cream and wine or stock together.
5. Butter 4 ramekin dishes and layer the sweet potatoes in them with the cheese and the spinach mixture, then pour over the wine or stock and the cream. Bake for 25 – 30 minutes.

Note: you can make this in a larger dish for a light supper. You may also wish to add some crispy bacon with the spinach to make a more substantial dish.

Chris Rich
Market gardener, near Bath

Chris Rich comes from a line of market gardeners that goes back to 1810, and all have been based in and around Batheaston. His family moved into the house where he now lives when he was three months old, and his father used to lay him down at the end of a row of runner beans, while he picked the crop. His brother Gerald owns the much-loved greengrocer's shop in Larkhall.

We walked across the fields and even though it was late October, plenty of crops were still growing. The cavolo nero looked beautiful with its lush dark leaves, and there were rows of pumpkins and squash of all colours and sizes.

The work is done mainly by hand, as the area is hilly and unsuited to large machinery. Cut flowers sell well, and in the winter there are brightly coloured berries on the holly. Chris's father collected the berries when the land behind Eagle House was converted into a housing estate, and he planted them in rows at the edge of the fields. Eagle House had been home to those suffragettes who were arrested and imprisoned as a result of their political protests. The women used to plant trees with commemorative plaques, and they continue to be remembered in Chris Rich's fields.

It is evident that Chris loves his job, and he values being his own boss, working outside and seeing the end results of his labour. However, he also has a constant battle with pests of various kinds. The foxes and badgers try to get at his chickens, and the deer eat crops such as spinach, beetroot, currants and berries. Chris accepts this as part of the natural order and remains positive. He continues to expand, with a new poly-tunnel to grow lettuces and herbs through the winter.

There is a welcoming atmosphere at Chris's place, and he keeps beautiful Lavender Pekin chickens simply because children love them. There is also an aviary, with colourful birds including quails. The farm shop itself is very attractive, with paintings and cards by Chris's daughter Lucy, who studied landscape and garden design, as well as working at Kew Gardens as a senior botanical horticulturalist.

Chris uses traditional farming methods, with as few pesticides as possible. He found that the public prefer to buy vegetables that are both local and as organic as possible, so he has taken on the extra work of weeding by hand. The reward is in the marvellous freshness and flavour of his produce, which is valued all over Bath.

Email Address:
rich432@btinternet.com

Phone Number:
01225 859929

Address:
Sevenacres, Northend, Batheaston,
Bath, BA1 7HJ

Opening Times:
| Monday - Friday | 8.30am - 6pm |
| Saturday | 8.30am - 4pm |

Where to Buy:
Farm Shop
Bath Farmers' Market

Leek Cobbler
with walnuts

Ingredients:

25g butter
4 tablespoons extra virgin rapeseed oil
1 kg leeks, washed and sliced
2 large onions, finely sliced
1 teaspoon paprika
1 teaspoon sea salt
100g walnuts, fresh if possible, shelled
30g pickled walnuts
For the pastry:
375g potatoes
175g self raising flour
75g Cheddar cheese
150g butter, cut into small pieces
1 large free-range egg yolk
2-3 tablespoons freshly grated cheese for the top

Method:

1. Melt the butter and oil in a large frying pan.
2. Add the leeks, onions, paprika and salt and fry gently until softened (about 45 minutes)
3. Add the walnuts and cook for a further 5 minutes.
4. Add the pickled walnuts and check the seasoning. Turn the mixture into a large, shallow ovenproof dish.
5. Heat the oven to 180°c, gas 4.
6. Cook the potatoes then mash them. Leave to cool.
7. Sieve the flour into a food processor, and add the grated cheese and butter. Blend until it resembles breadcrumbs. Add the mashed potatoes. Roll out and cut circles. Use these to cover the leek and walnut layer. Brush this with the egg yolk, and sprinkle with the grated cheese. Bake for 30-40 minutes.

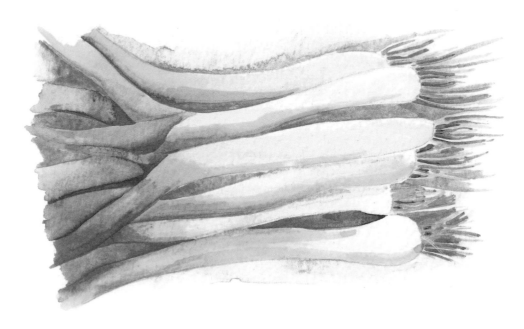

PJ's Farm
Pig farmers, near Bath

PJ's farm is run by Jamie and his father Mike. The whole family is highly entrepreneurial, running a beef farm alongside a livery yard and a bookselling business.

PJ's farm started as an experiment in 2004: Jamie and Mike started to rear British Lop pigs and found that they were ideally suited to their situation, and are unusual in that they can eat a far wider range of foods than most pigs. The family has started to grow their own barley, and the pigs love it, along with left over fruit and vegetables from the local greengrocers.

Grassland is very important in an area that has heavy clay soil. It helps with drainage, as it allows earthworms to flourish. If pigs are allowed to root freely, they destroy the structure of the soil. For this reason the sows are fitted with a nose ring, and the piglets are reared in an open yard once they have been weaned at ten weeks (most farmers only give them three weeks).

Jamie and Mike decided against going with the 'farm assured' scheme, as it would have meant giving up the use of their local abattoir. It is vital for the animals to be allowed a stress-free environment, and a longer journey would have been traumatic for them. Animal welfare is paramount on this farm.

The pigs have a good life, reared in small groups with plenty of space to move around, and they have six months instead of the usual four. The positive feedback from customers is proof that this works, as the flavour of their meat is excellent. Their biggest problem is matching supply to demand. They are turning down requests for regular orders from restaurants, as they are aware that if they expand their business too fast, they may lose the quality of product that has made their brand so successful.

Their focus is very much on local connections. They have been involved in a project at Beechen Cliff School, in which they donated a pig for the school to rear, and then to slaughter and process. The school chef cooked the resulting sausages, and the rest of the meat was sold (to the staff, who loved it) to provide the funding to buy another pig. They are proud to be keeping this rare breed going, and to be informing a new generation about the importance of quality in meat production.

Website Address:
www.pjs-farm.co.uk

Email address:
mail@pjs-farm.co.uk

Address:
c/o Copperfield Farm,
Marshfield Lane, Beach,
Bristol, BS30 6NP

Opening Times:
All day Fridays and Saturdays

Where to Buy:
PJs Farm Stall, Green Park, Bath
The Tollshed, Tollgate Inn, Holt.

Pork Fillet
with halloumi and redcurrant jelly

Ingredients:

400 - 600g pork fillet
4 teaspoons redcurrant jelly
100g halloumi, grated
20g butter
150ml crème fraìche
20g Old Ford cheese from Sleight Farm,
cut into slithers. You could also use
Parmesan or Pecorino

Method:

1. Cut the pork fillet into eight pieces, and wrap individually in clingfilm.
    Gently hammer each so that it is evenly flattened.
2. Season each fillet, then spread over the redcurrant jelly and the halloumi.
3. Roll up each fillet, and place in a buttered baking dish.
4. Cut up the butter and sprinkle over the fillet rolls.
5. Cover with foil and cook in a low oven, 150°c, gas 2, for about an hour.
6. Pour the cooking juices from the meat into a pan, and stir in the crème fraìche.
7. Slice the meat and arrange on a dish.
8. Spoon the juices over the meat and scatter with the cheese.
9. Serve with lightly steamed or griddled asparagus, which is in season.

Brown & Forrest Smokery

Smokery, Somerset

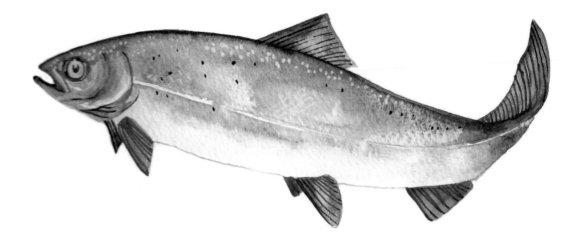

Brown and Forrest is a small family business, established in the early 1980s. They learnt to smoke fish in Germany, then returned to Somerset to set up their own small wood-fired system. You can take a guided tour to see the whole process, which is surprisingly simple.

Fish and meat are cured in salt and brown sugar for up to six days. It is then left to settle in the fridge for a couple of days. They are smoked flat rather than hung, as this produces a better texture: it is moist, but with a bite to it.

Some foods are hot smoked which involves a form of slow cooking over a log fire. When the food is cooked through, wood chippings are added and the food is left for a couple of hours to smoke. This works particularly well for chicken, duck and trout.

In cold smoking, the food is not cooked. A circular trail of oak sawdust is laid out on the floor and then embers are used to light one end. This produces smoke but no flames and limited heat. Smoking times vary depending on the food being smoked. I was told that it is possible to smoke different foods at the same time, as there is no cross-contamination of flavour. This is ideal for salmon, trout, haddock, hams or cheese.

Different types of wood chippings are used depending on what is being smoked, but oak chippings are used for most foods, including salmon.

The focus is on enhancing the flavour of the food. For example, when smoking Jamie Montgomery's Cheddar for Neal's Yard they add a strength of taste that complements the intensity of the cheese. More often, however, they aim for subtlety.

Website Address:
www.smokedeel.co.uk

Phone Number:
01458 250875

Email Address:
info@smokedeel.co.uk

Address:
Bowdens Farm Smokery, Hambridge, Somerset, TA10 0BP

Opening Times:
Monday - Saturday   10am - 4pm

Where to Buy:
Online
Their own shop

Where to Eat:
At their own restaurant.

Smoked Salmon Tart
with sundried tomatoes and horseradish

Ingredients:

For the pastry:
170g plain flour
110g butter
1 free-range egg yolk

For the filling:
15g butter
1 large onion, chopped finely
1 clove garlic, crushed
100g sundried tomatoes in oil, sliced
170g smoked salmon
150ml single cream, soured cream or
crème fraîche
3 teaspoons creamed horseradish
2 eggs
Grated nutmeg
1 tablespoon fresh breadcrumbs
1 tablespoon grated cheese

Method:

1. To make the pastry, sieve the flour into a bowl with a pinch of sea salt. Rub in the butter until it is evenly mixed (like breadcrumbs). Add the egg yolk and mix to a dough. Leave in the fridge in a plastic bag or container for 30 minutes.
2. Heat the oven to 180°, gas 4.
3. Butter a dish (25cm acros) and line with the pastry. The pastry is very short, so has a tendency to break up. Just press the pastry pieces onto the dish, then prick with a fork. Chill in the fridge for at least 20 minutes.
4. Line the flan dish with greaseproof paper, then add some rice or lentils to 'bake blind' for 15 minutes (this stops the pastry from puffing up). Remove the greaseproof paper, rice or lentils from the flan and return to the oven for a further 5 minutes.
5. Turn the oven down to 150°c, gas 2.
6. Meanwhile, fry the onion in the butter and a tablespoon of oil from the sundried tomatoes. Cook for 20 minutes then add the sundried tomatoes and onion. Mix well and allow to cool.
7. Spread the tomato and onion mixture over the base of the flan, then put the smoked salmon on top.
8. Mix the cream, horseradish and eggs together. Season with nutmeg, sea salt and freshly ground black pepper.
9. Pour this over the smoked salmon, then top with the cheese and breadcrumbs.
10. Bake 30 minutes until golden.
11. Serve with seasonal purple sprouting broccoli. This is good hot or cold.

Vowley Farm
Beef farmers in Wiltshire

When Lorraine and Mark Stanton decided to move to the countryside their main interest was in working with horses. However, the land they found was specifically agricultural, so they decided to shift their focus.

They bought a small herd of British White cattle, and applied many of the principles that they had learned through working with horses. They wanted the cattle to be able to eat the food that they would instinctively choose, living in a natural environment. They found that cows like to live communally, rather than in the separate cubicles that most farms use, and they like to have access to the outside.

They manage the pasture so as to encourage the wild flowers, which create diversity of grazing for the cows. Cows are naturally ruminants, eating grass and a range of plants that grow in the hedgerows: 'A holistic approach to farming is more soulful, nurturing the soul of life.'

Lorraine and Mark's animals live longer, eat good food and are allowed to range free, so are more expensive to raise: 'You input your heart and soul and passion, and this is what makes the produce taste so wonderful.'

People are increasingly aware of the advantages of eating meat that has been raised with care, so they have a loyal customer base, but economic pressures mean that people are buying less – only a third of what they bought two years ago.

Lorraine and Mark also raise Gloucester Old Spot pigs, which live in family groups, and who are able to mix peaceably with the cows once they are big enough. When the pigs go to the abattoir, in pairs in a straw-filled trailer, they fall asleep within minutes of setting off. There is no stress at all – a peaceful end to a tranquil existence.

The 110 acre farm is a picture of harmony. The bull is anything but fierce, grazing happily, surrounded by his 'harem'. Liberated battery chickens roam around the farmyard, eating insects that they find and in this way keeping everything clean and clear. They lay their eggs in a shed where they sleep at night to keep safe from foxes.

Website Address:
www.vowleyfarm.co.uk

Phone Number:
01793 852115

Email Address:
us@vowleyfarm.co.uk

Address:
Binknoll Lane,
Wootton Bassett,
Wiltshire, SN4 8QR

Opening Times:
Thursday   3pm - 7pm

Where to Buy:
Farmers' Markets in Swindon, Devizes and Wootton Bassett

Fillet steaks, Rossini style
Originally created in honour of the composer, Rossini

Ingredients:

1 tablespoon butter
2 tablespoons extra virgin rapeseed oil
4 slices of beef fillet, about 200g each
4 sliced mushrooms
3-4 garlic cloves, finely sliced
100g young spinach leaves
2 tablespoons Somerset cider brandy
100ml stock
4 slices of smooth duck or chicken pâté
4 slices of sourdough bread, without the
crust, toasted (about the same size as
the meat)

Method:

1. Heat half the butter and the oil in a hot frying pan.
2. Season the fillet steaks with sea salt and freshly ground black pepper and cook over a high heat for 2- 3 minutes on each side until the steaks are crusted on the outside but rare inside. Remove from the pan and set aside.
3. Add the rest of the butter and oil to the pan and fry the mushrooms for a few minutes, then add the garlic and spinach. Allow the spinach to wilt, then remove from the pan and keep warm.
4. Deglaze the pan with the Somerset cider brandy and the stock. Allow this sauce to reduce in volume.
5. Presentation: spread each slice of toast with some pâté, then place a steak fillet on top of each. Arrange the mushrooms and spinach round the edges. Drizzle with the sauce. Serve immediately.

French Style Peas:

50 g butter
6 spring onions, finely chopped
8 outside lettuce leaves, shredded
500g peas (frozen are fine for this)
2 sprigs mint
2 teaspoons sugar
Sea salt and freshly ground black pepper
4 tablespoons stock

Method:

1. Melt the butter in a saucepan and gently fry the spring onions until soft.
2. Add the lettuce leaves and stir over a low heat.
3. Add the peas, mint, sugar. Season with sea salt and freshly ground black pepper.
4. Pour in the stock, cover tightly, and cook over a gentle heat for 10 minutes or so until the peas are tender.

Hurdlebrook Dairy
Guernsey milk and cream producers in Somerset

Dave Paul's family has been raising Guernsey cows for two generations. His grandfather brought them over from Guernsey, and his mother used to do the milking. Dave's enthusiasm is infectious, as he talks about his 'cracking cows' that give such excellent quality milk.

Dave and his wife, Rosie, have recently laid tracks for the cows to get out into the pastures as early as possible in the spring, without getting muddy udders or damaging the pasture. The tracks are made of reclaimed concrete sleepers, in keeping with their desire for as much sustainability as possible on their farm.

The milk is unpasteurised, which means that you get a full flavour along with silky creaminess. It is truly delicious milk and cream, as I discovered when I was given some to take home to try out. I shall never buy skimmed milk again, especially as it not only lacks flavour, but also the fat-soluble vitamins (A, D, E and K) contained in the cream.

The cream is fabulous in puddings, but also in savoury dishes; as Rosie pointed out, it is so thick that it makes a sauce on its own.

The yoghurt contains no preservatives, potato starch, skimmed milk powder or other thickeners. It is just milk and culture, and has body because of the quality of the milk. All the containers are sealed with the old fashioned crimped edge – a detail that gives a pleasurable sense of tradition.

Rosie says that in the last five years she has really noticed a change in people's attitudes, as they increasingly want to know the origins of their food.

They have plenty of outlets for their milk, cream and yoghurts. They sell to some London markets where the different ethnic groups use their products in new ways that Dave finds fascinating. Neal's Yard also sells their products, which is a real accolade.

Website Address:
www.hurdlebrook.co.uk

Westcombe Dairy:
Overton Farm,
Babcary, Somerton,
Somerset TA11 7EJ

Phone Number:
01458 223229

Email Address:
info@hurdlebrook.co.uk

Opening Times: N/A

Where to Buy:
Frome Farmers' Market
www.localfooddirect.co.uk

Crème Brûlée
for total indulgence

Ingredients:

1 litre double cream
1 vanilla pod, slit open lengthways
6 free-range egg yolks
200g caster sugar

Method:

1. Place the cream in a saucepan. Scrape the seeds from the vanilla pod and add the seeds and the pod to the cream. Bring to boiling point and turn off the heat. Leave to cool for about 10 minutes, then strain the liquid into a jug.
2. Meanwhile, place the yolks and half the caster sugar in a bowl and mix.
3. Gently pour the warm cream onto the sugar and egg yolk mixture, and mix well.
4. Butter an ovenproof dish (about 26cm) and pour in the mixture.
5. Bake in a bain-marie for an hour at 120°c, gas 1. Remove the dish from the bain-marie and allow to cool. Chill in the fridge for at least 2 hours.
6. Sprinkle the rest of the sugar over the top of the pudding to cover completely. Put the dish under a very hot grill for about 5 minutes, turning it round and checking to ensure that it does not burn. The top should start to turn brown. If you have a blowtorch, you can use it to complete the browning process, ensuring every part of the top is caramelised. It should be hard and crisp. You can tap the top with a spoon to check this.
7. Chill in the fridge for another hour, then serve.

Homewood Cheeses
Artisan cheese maker, The Mendips

Tim Homewood has worked as a cheese maker with Graham Padfield of Bath Soft Cheese, and Mary Holbrook at Sleight Farm. He says that 'she is a great influence on those who want to get into handmade artisan cheeses'. Tim's main cheese is the very delicious Old Demdike, a semi-hard cheese. He also makes a marinated sheep's cheese (for which he uses Fussels sunflower oil), which can be used in the same way as a feta. His halloumi is much sought after and ricotta is produced as a delicious side-product.

Tim met Angela Morris at a farmers' market where she had a stall selling her cakes and preserves. Now she is helping to market Tim's cheeses. She is an excellent cook, and I was lucky enough to be given a delicious lunch of her parsnip and leek soup, home-made cheesy flatbreads and her famous cheesecake. She used to make cheesecakes so as not to waste the spare cheese, but now they have to make cheese especially. Her cheesecakes are much in demand at Bath and Bristol Farmers' Markets.

In my cheesecake I have used Tim's lovely 'fresh' ewe's cheese, which is like a curd cheese, but contains a starter. This kind of cheese is well-known in many parts of the world, but in England not many people have come across it. In Scotland it is called 'crowdie', and in the past was known as 'peasant's cheese' because everyone used to make it. It is a simple, useable everyday cheese, and Tim has chosen to put it into small re-usable containers to make it easier to transport.

Website Address:
www.homewoodcheeses.co.uk

Phone Numbers:
01761 241413
07816 447242

Email Address:
info@homewoodcheeses.co.uk

Address and Opening Times: N/A

Where to Buy:
Bath Farmer's Market
Bristol Farmer's Market
Dick Willows Farm Shop, Bathford
Paxton and Whitfield, Bath
Larkhall Butchers,Bath
Neston Park Farm Shop, Atworth

Ginger Cheesecake
with a ginger biscuit base

Ingredients:

200g good quality ginger biscuits
50g butter
250g fresh ewe's cheese or cream cheese
2 free-range eggs
1 lemon
50g caster sugar
4 pieces of stem ginger in syrup
200ml crème fraîche or d ouble cream

Method:

1. Heat the oven to 180°c, gas 4.
2. Crush the biscuits in a strong bag, using a rolling pin.
3. Melt the butter in a pan then add the biscuits. Stir well. Press this mixture into a well-buttered cake tin with a loose base, and spread evenly.
4. Combine the cheese with the eggs, lemon zest and juice and the sugar. Pour this mixture over the biscuit base. Bake in the oven for 30 minutes.
5. Blend the stem ginger in a food processor with the crème fraîche or whipped double cream, so that the ginger is broken into small pieces. Add 2 tablespoons of the ginger syrup. Pour this over the cheesecake, then return to the oven for 15 minutes. Turn the oven off, but leave the cheesecake in the oven to cool. I decorated it with slices of caramelised lemon (boiled in water and sugar).

Bath Harvest Extra Virgin Rapeseed Oils
Rapeseed oil producer, near Bath

Debbie Brown is a great enthusiast for British rapeseed oil. She lives in a cottage with her family just 200 yards away from Wilmington Farm, a Duchy estate of 600 acres, where the rapeseed is grown. She is having a farm building converted so that she can install her own press, as she has been using a contract presser to produce her oil. She is keen to reduce the food miles that this involves, as well as wanting eventually to have a centre where visitors can experience the process.

Debbie has held stalls at the Tobacco Factory Market and 'Love Food' Festivals such as the one held at Dyrham Park, where I first came across her product.

One approach to promoting her oil is to use it to make delicious chocolate brownies, and she gives samples to people to demonstrate how the mild flavour is well suited to use in baking. I was given a taste of her cranberry and chocolate brownies, which were both dairy-free and gluten-free and wonderfully light.

The flavour of Bath Harvest rapeseed oil has been compared to walnut oil, so is ideal in salads, but it can be used for most recipes where you would usually use olive oil. The main advantages of rapeseed oil are that it is very low in saturated fat, contains ten times more omega 3 and has a higher burn-point compared to olive oil.

Debbie's cold-pressed rapeseed oil won bronze in the 2012 Taste of the West.and she has also introduced a range of oils infused with chilli, garlic or lemon.

Bath Harvest Rapeseed Oil is truly local to Bath. Debbie started in September 2011, and her entrepreneurial skills should be rewarded by a warm response from food enthusiasts.

Website Address:
www.bathharvestoils.co.uk

Phone Numbers:
01373 831286
07967 220606

Email Address:
gary@fusselsfinefoods.co.uk

Address:
Wilmington Farm, Bath, BA2 9JB

Where to Buy:
Dick Willows, Bathford
PJs Farm Stall, Green Park, Bath
Hartleys Farm Shop, Bradford on Avon
Newton Farm Shop, Newton St Loe
The Tasting Room, Green Street, Bath
Eades Greengrocers, Julian Road, Bath

Queen of Sheba Cake
A dairy-free chocolate cake (but lovely with double cream!)

Ingredients:

100g good quality dark chocolate
100g extra virgin rapeseed oil
2 free-range eggs
100g sugar
45g self raising flour
A pinch of sea salt

For the topping
50g good quality dark chocolate

Method:

1. Melt the chocolate gently with the oil in a bowl over a pan of hot water.
2. Beat the egg yolks with the sugar until creamy (keep the whites for later)
3. Add the chocolate and oil to the egg yolks and sugar. Mix well. (Do not wash the bowl as you can use it to melt the chocolate for the topping).
4. Fold in the sieved flour, and salt.
5. Whisk the egg whites until stiff, then fold into the mixture.
6. Pour into a lightly oiled heat-proof bowl or cake tin (18cm).
7. Bake at 180°c, gas 4 for 45-50 minutes.
8. Cool before turning out.
9. Top with melted chocolate.

Avalon Vineyard
Pennard organic wines and cider, Somerset

Hugh and Hilary Tripp originally bought a cottage with a garden in East Pennard thirty years ago, wanting to escape from London where Hugh worked in biological research.

He spotted an abandoned barrel on a street in Soho, and when it was still there a few days later, he decided to bring it with him to Somerset, where he used it for many years to make cider.

He speaks fondly of the cider making process, which he says is 'the simplest of them all', involving as little intervention as possible. His press came from a local farm, is sturdy looking and virtually an antique. He has pressed apples with his neighbor Michael Eavis, and still enjoys the Glastonbury festival where he sells a great deal of his cider, as well as his organic mead - the only one made in the west country - which is popular throughout the year in Glastonbury itself.

Gradually Hugh and Hilary bought up surrounding fields, and started a 'pick your own' fruit business. This didn't really work, so they decided to make wine out of the fruit. This has been extremely successful, as Hugh's natural instinct was to grow without spraying, even before the organic movement became widespread. They planted vines in the early 1980s, and again resisted the common practice of spraying against mildew. They were fortunate in having chosen vines that are hybrids, resistant to mildew, and from the outset their crops were abundant. In 2006 the Social Association awarded them organic status, and they have received a gold medal in the Regional Taste of the West for their Pennard Raspberry Liqueur. All fruit wines are made with their own fruit – none is imported.

They built the winery, and from then on carried out all of the processes themselves, with help at busy times from WOOFers, volunteers who work at weekends on organic farms. They are unpaid, but are given food and accommodation.

Hugh gave us a taste of his dry white wine and it was delicious.

Website Address:
www.avalonvineyard.co.uk
www.pennardorganicwines

Phone Number:
01749 860393

Email Address:
Htripp@avalonvineyard.co.uk

Address:
The Drove,
East Pennard, Shepton Mallet
Somerset, BA4 6UA

Opening Times (Barn):
Guided tours are available by prior arrangement; self guided tours and tastings are free.

Where to Buy:
Order online
www.localfooddirect.co.uk
Dick Willows, Bathford
Harvest, Bath
Prior Park Garden Centre, Bath
Nibbles Cheese, Guildhall Market, Bath

Rhubarb in Mead
with a creamy topping

Ingredients:

800g rhubarb, washed and cut into rough
pieces
200ml mead
50g honey
200g cream cheese
100g caster sugar
2 free-range eggs, separated
300ml double cream
2 free-range egg whites
75g caster sugar

Method:

1.   Put the rhubarb, mead and honey in a saucepan and simmer gently for 30 -40
     minutes. Pour into a baking dish (about 22cm across), and allow to cool.
      This is quite tart in flavour, but the sweetness of the topping balances it out.
2.   Beat the cream cheese with the sugar. Add the egg yolks and cream. Mix well.
3.   Whisk the four egg whites in a bowl with a pinch of salt, until soft peaks have
     formed. Fold carefully into the cream mixture. Pour this carefully over the
     cooled rhubarb, and bake in the oven at 170°c, gas 3, for 25 minutes.
     Allow to cool, then place it, uncovered, in the fridge for a couple of hours.
4.   Sprinkle the sugar over the top of the cream mixture, then put under a hot grill
     to turn golden or use a blow torch. Chill in the fridge for at least an hour to set.

Rhubarb grows best in cold, wet conditions. However, much rhubarb is forced or grown
indoors, making it more tender.
British rhubarb becomes available in February. Champagne rhubarb is one of the
earliest crops and needs quite a bit of sugar as it is fairly tart in flavour. By May, rhubarb
is a darker colour, with a sharp flavour.

Summer

Castle Farm
Organic fruit and vegetable farmers, Bath

Jo and Eileen are used to hard work. Last year they gave up their annual trip to Glastonbury, as it clashed with the raspberry harvest. Even during a trip to a festival they are fully employed with their festival artwork, which is stored in their barn, overflowing with gloriously colourful and creative objects.

They grow a splendid array of fruit, vegetables and herbs, and supply various restaurants in the area. They are also involved in box schemes and some farmers' markets.

The valley is very fertile, and had been unused for fifteen years before they started to farm it. They have a herd of cattle, fortunate animals who are allowed to range around the beautiful landscape in a semi-wild state.

Jo came to Bath from a farming background in Wales. She has fifty acres, which stretch down to a river, and she describes it as 'heaven on earth'. Her ideal would be to build an ecohouse in the valley.

The polytunnels and outside growing areas are bursting with a great variety of produce. They use manure from the cows, as well as a system of mulching, so the plants are wonderfully healthy.

In 1998 Castle Farm became a member of the Soil Association, and achieved full organic status in 2000. Jo specialises in edible flowers for salads, such as borage, nasturtiums, geraniums and marigolds. It is marvellous to see such a consumable area of colour and beauty.

Website Address:
www.castlefarmorganics.co.uk

Phone Number:
01225 840244

Email address:
enquiries@castlefarmorganics.co.uk

Address:
Castle Farm, Midford,
Bath, BA2 7BU

Opening Times: N/A

Where to Buy:
From the farm gate and a few local outlets
Harvest, Bath

Where to eat:
Demuths, North Parade Passage, Bath
The Circus, Brock Street, Bath

38

Summer Salad
with spinach and herbs

Ingredients:

8 small tomatoes
16 small basil leaves
2 cloves of garlic, finely sliced
4 tablespoons extra virgin rapeseed oil
1 small aubergine, sliced (or you could use a bulb of fennel)
2 shallots, very thinly sliced
2 teaspoons mustard
2 teaspoons runny honey
1 tablespoon cider vinegar
200g baby spinach leaves
20g flat leaf parsley
20g chives
100g soft cheese such as Bath Soft Cheese
20g edible flowers such as nasturtiums, if available

Method:

1. Halve the tomatoes, sprinkle with sea salt and press a basil leaf and a slice of garlic into each half. Place them in a low oven, around 110°c, gas ▢ for a couple of hours. This really concentrates the flavour.
2. Heat half the oil in a frying pan and gently fry the aubergine (or fennel) until soft and golden. Remove from the pan, then fry the shallots until crisp in the same pan.
3. Mix the rest of the oil with the mustard, honey and vinegar and add to the pan.
4. Arrange the spinach and herbs on a large plate. Place the aubergine (or fennel) and shallot mixture over the leaves, with the tomatoes on top. Crumble the cheese over the top. Drizzle with a little of the herb oil (below) and decorate with the edible flowers, if available.

Herb Oil:

20g of fresh herbs such as basil or chives
6 tablespoons extra virgin rapeseed oil
Half a teaspoon sea salt
A little freshly ground black pepper

Method:

Blend the ingredients until a smooth purée is formed. This will keep in a jar in the fridge for a couple of weeks.

Natural Woodland Pigs
Pig farmers, North Somerset

Andrew Sartain has taken on the management of thirty acres of woodland in which he is rearing Tamworth pigs. Every group of six piglets has an acre or more of woodland to range in, which means that their habitat can withstand their foraging. This is partly because of the amount of space they have, but also because the woodland is based on limestone, which is too hard for the pigs to damage.

The piglets live in structures made by Andrew out of hazel, coppiced from the surrounding woodland. They live for about eight months and finally they are taken to the local abattoir only two miles away, in the Langford Veterinary School.

Andrew is an expert in both butchery and charcuterie, making European-style sausages. He has degrees in agriculture and sustainable forestry as well as having been a Michelin-starred chef.

This is certainly an example of sustainability and animal husbandry at its best, and it's a relief to be able to buy pork without any confusion as to whether the pig has genuinely spent its life outdoors.

Web Site Address:
www.thewildfoodlarder.co.uk

Phone Number:
07772 398957 (daytime)
01934 838217 (evenings)

Email address:
andrew@the wildfoodlarder.co.uk

Where to Buy:
Order online
Farmers' Markets in Bath,
Wrington and Redland Markets, Bristol

The Upton Cheyney Chilli Company
Chilli growers, Gloucestershire

Alex and Louise started their chilli farm in 2008, with Louise producing their award winning range of sauces in the kitchen of the farm shop. The smell is glorious!

Alex is in charge of the farming and the care of the chillies. He has a romantic side, which led him to grow chillies for their beauty.

Manor Farm is of 'special scientific interest', and was mentioned in the Doomsday Book. People are encouraged to visit during the growing season (March to November), and children are welcome.

The chillies, and many of the other ingredients used in the sauces, are grown without the use of pesticides on Manor Farm. They use Fussels extra virgin rapeseed oil for their flavoured oils. They have their own smokehouse, in which the chillies are cold-smoked over oak chippings for 18 hours. When a jalapeno chilli is smoked it becomes a chipotle.

Clearly Alex's approach works, as not only do Barts spices use his chillies, but also their Oak Smoke Chipottle sauce won gold in 2012 at both the Great Taste Awards and the Taste of the West.

Website Address:
www.uptonchilli.co.uk

Email address:
sales@uptonchilli.co.uk

Address:
Manor Farm, Upton Cheyney
Bristol, BS30 6NQ

Opening Times:
Friday - Sunday   10am - 6pm

Where to Buy:
Manor Farm shop
Dick Willows, Bathford
www.localfooddirect.co.uk

Sausage meatballs
with chilli tomato chutney

Ingredients:

200g tomatoes
A handful of fresh thyme leaves
2 tablespoons extra virgin rapeseed oil
3 large shallots, chopped
2 large cloves of garlic, crushed with a
teaspoon of coarse sea salt
1 teaspoon Upton Cheyney mango, lime
and red habanero sauce
2 tablespoons flat leaf parsley, chopped
400g sausages
A little flour, seasoned with sea salt and
freshly ground black pepper
120 ml red wine

Method:

1. Heat the oven to 180°c, gas 4.
2. To make the chilli tomato chutney, halve the tomatoes, and sprinkle a few thyme leaves on each with some sea salt and freshly ground black pepper. Place them on an oiled ovenproof baking tray and roast in the oven for 30 minutes. Allow tocool, then remove the skins.
3. Heat 1 tablespoon of the oil. Fry the shallots for 5 minutes.
4. Add the garlic, and fry gently for a further 5 minutes.
5. Add the tomatoes (with any juices from the pan), the chilli sauce and most of the parsley, and check the seasoning. Mix well and remove from the heat.
6. Meanwhile, in another pan, heat the remaining oil.
7. Remove the sausage skin and divide the meat into small balls. Roll each in some seasoned flour.
8. Fry the sausage balls until golden on all sides – about 15 minutes.
9. Add the wine and cook until it has evaporated.
10. Serve the sausage balls with the chilli tomato chutney, sprinkled with the remaining parsley.

Arcadia Organics
Organic fruit and vegetables - near Bristol

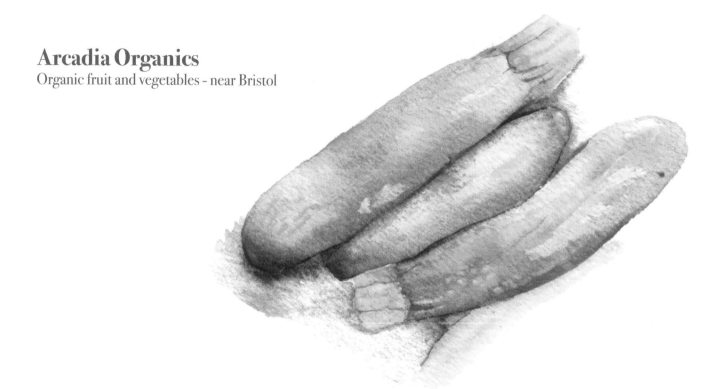

Phelim Knifton and his mother Rosey started growing organic fruit and vegetables on their twenty acres of land in 1996. To begin with they lived in the village, then they moved to a mobile home on the land. In 2005 they built a lovely farmhouse, where I was given a delicious lunch of home made bread and cheese, with some of their glorious salad leaves.

Everything about the place shows an awareness of environmental issues, from the solar panels on the roof of the house, to the copses of native trees and the abundant hedgerows, which have been carefully preserved.

They have a large greenhouse and ten polytunnels, as well as an orchard with fifty fruit trees. They grow a wide range of fruit and vegetables, and you can rely on everything being both top quality and organic.

An ongoing problem is the destruction of crops by slugs, especially the tender salad leaves and pak choi that they grow. Phelim uses organic products to tackle issues of this kind, but in the end it comes down to the manual removal of pests.

I discovered that it is important to buy salad leaves that are not presented in sealed containers or 'modified atmosphere packaging', which aims to lengthen the shelf life of salads. In fact this process reduces vital nutrients (**British Journal of Nutrition 2003**). It is good to know that when you buy from Arcadia Organics, you are eating a product that is not only delicious, but also healthy.

Website Address:
www.arcadiaorganics.com

Phone Number:
01934 876886

Email address:
rosey@arcadiaorganics.com

Address:
Clover Nursery, Streamcross,
Lower Claverham, North Somerset
 BS49 4QA

Opening Times (Barn):
Fridays   1pm - 6pm

Where to Buy:
Bath Farmers' Market

Mini Courgette Bakes
with hazel nuts or cob nuts

Ingredients:

30ml extra virgin rapeseed oil
1 onion, finely chopped
100g hazelnuts or cob nuts, chopped
500g courgettes, chopped
2 teaspoons cumin seeds
20g fresh turmeric (peeled weight)
or 2 teaspoons powdered turmeric.
2 teaspoons grated ginger
75g rolled oats
75g ground nuts, such as almonds or
cashews
100g coconut cream
1 teaspoon paprika
200g tomatoes, peeled and chopped (you
can use tinned tomatoes)

Method:

1. Heat half the rapeseed oil in a large frying pan, then add the onion. Fry for a few minutes, then add the hazelnuts or cob nuts and courgettes. Cook, stirring, for about 10 minutes.
2. Heat the oven to 180°c, gas 4.
3. Heat the rest of the oil in a small frying pan, then add the cumin, turmeric and ginger and fry gently for a few minutes. Mix with the courgettes and nuts.
4. Add the oats, ground nuts, tomatoes, coconut cream and paprika, then season to taste with sea salt and freshly ground black pepper.
5. Grease four large ramekins and pour in the mixture. Bake for 15 - 20 minutes until the tops are brown.

Note: You can make this in a larger dish for a delicious light supper

43

Artisan Somerset Cheese
Cheddar cheese makers

Somerset is famous for its Cheddar cheese, but the name is not protected, so anyone making this type of cheese can use the term. For this reason a group of farmers based in the South West of England joined together to gain 'Protected Designation of Origin' (PDO) status, with the title West Country Farmhouse Cheese. Cheese can only be called this if it is made from raw or pasteurised milk from local herds, with no added preservatives or colouring. Cheese must be made in Somerset, Dorset, Devon or Cornwall, using traditional methods and must be matured on the farm for at least nine months in traditional cloth-wrapped cylinders or blocks.

In 2002, the Slow Food Movement endorsed the establishment of the Artisan Somerset Cheddar Presidium to protect and promote the few remaining traditional raw milk producers in this country. Randolph Hodgson, the proprietor of Neal's Yard Dairy, became the co-ordinator of Slow Food's Cheddar Presidium. So far, it has three members: Montgomery's, Westcombe and Keen's Cheddar. Each farm has its own microclimate, which means that every farm produces milk and cheese that is subtly different in its flavour. Keen's has a very strong core to its flavour, Westcombe is mellow, with a length to its taste, and Montgomery's is dry, fruity and complex.

Westcombe Dairy:
Tom Calver's family has been making cheese in Westcombe village since 1890. In the early 1990s they decided to return to traditional methods and the original recipes of the 1890s. They grow 80-90% of the cows' feed, including maize, grass silage and wheat. The quality of the feed has a huge impact on the flavour of the cheese. Tom is often at Bath Farmers' Market. His knowledge about cheesemaking and his enthusiasm for his product are inspirational. Winner of Best Cheddar at Bath and West Show 2011.

Keen's Cheddar:
The Keen family has been making cheese for generations, and it is this sense of heritage that enables them to produce their top quality Cheddar. For George the best thing about his job is talking to people who have an involvement in all issues related to cheese. This varies from rediscovering some of the original flavours of our classic cheeses to an enthusiasm for emerging new cheeses. He remembers when there was a very limited number of cheeses in this country, and is positive about the opportunities that are arising for small producers to develop new and individual products. His focus is on authenticity, which is what makes his Cheddar so unique.

Montgomery's Cheddar:
Jamie Montgomery uses a peg mill for milling the curd, which is responsible for its slightly broken texture. The cheese is allowed to mature for eighteen months. As demand exceeds production, it is only available at a very few outlets, such as Paxton and Whitfield in Bath.

Website Address:
www.slowfood.org.uk/artisan-somerset-cheddar

Westcombe Dairy:
Lower Westcombe Farm,
Evercreech, Shepton Mallet,
Somerset. BA4 6ER

Keen's Cheddar:
Moorhayes Farm,
Verrington Lane, Wincanton,
Somerset BA9 8JR.

Montgomrey's Cheddar:
Manor Farm,
Yeovil, Somerset

Where to Buy:
From their own farms
Dick Willows, Bathford
Chandos Delis, Bath
Fine Cheese Company, Bath
Paxton and Whitfield, Bath
Newton Farm Shop, Newton St Loe, Bath
Neston Park Farm Shop, Atworth.

Where to Eat:
The Longs Arms, South Wraxall

Stuffed Mushrooms
with Cheddar cheese topping

Ingredients:

4 large Portabella mushrooms
4 teaspoons extra virgin rapeseed oil

For the filling:
1 tomato, finely chopped
Half a red chilli, de-seeded and finely chopped
1 shallot, finely chopped
Half a red pepper, finely chopped
3-4 anchovies, finely chopped
4 large green olives, stones removed and finely chopped
1 clove of garlic, finely chopped
1 teaspoon capers, rinsed and finely chopped
Zest and juice of half an unwaxed lime
2 teaspoons cider vinegar
80g grated Cheddar cheese
30g chopped fresh parsley or coriander (you can use the stalks)
50g fresh breadcrumbs

For the topping:
40g grated Cheddar cheese

Method:

1. Combine all the ingredients for the filling.
2. Place the mushrooms in a buttered ovenproof dish, and season with sea salt and freshly ground black pepper.
3. Divide the filling between the mushrooms. Top with the rest of the cheese.
4. Bake in the oven at 180°c, gas 4, for 20 – 30 minutes, depending on the size of the mushrooms.

Note: if you can't find an unwaxed lime, you can pour boiling water over the fruit, which will help to remove some of the wax.

Bath City Farm
Community farm, central Bath

Twerton Hill Farm pre-dates the Doomsday Book of the 11th century. It has been farmed for 10,000 years, and in the 1990s it was taken over as a community project. In 1995 it became a charity. They rely on donations, and have no direct funding from the council – in fact they pay them rent. They always need volunteers, who work in the vegetable patch as well as helping with the animals.

The farm owns a Gloucester Old Spot, and two Kune Kune pigs (the smallest domesticated type of pig in the world, popular because of their friendly habits and the fact that they are very easy to manage). The piglets live in idyllic conditions for six months, and breeders live for three and a half years, with regular visits from a boar.

I was told that it is difficult to be sure whether a pig has had a decent life from the system of labelling in this country. For example, 'outdoor reared' may still involve the mothers being kept in farrowing crates. The only real way is to visit the farm yourself so that you can see the conditions they live in. Unfortunately a number of the major supermarkets force the farmers to cut corners in order to keep prices down.

The aim of Bath City Farm is to raise awareness of the environment, sustainability and animal welfare, serving as an example of how animals should be reared. I recommend you to visit them and to buy some of their excellent meat.

Website Address:
www.bathcityfarm.org.uk

Phone Number:
01225 481269

Address:
Kelston View
Bath
BA2 1NW

Opening Times:
Monday - Saturday   9am - 5pm

Where to Buy:
Bath Farmers' Market, the first Saturday of each month.

Pork Patties
with spring onions

Ingredients:

For the patties:
400g minced pork
100g fresh breadcrumbs
7-8 spring onions, chopped
2 cloves garlic, finely chopped
20g parsley leaves, chopped
2 teaspoons finely grated ginger
1 free-range egg
Juice and zest of a lime
1 teaspoon ground coriander seed
2 teaspoons paprika
1 teaspoon sea salt

To fry the patties:
 2 tablespoons extra virgin rapeseed oil.

To serve:
Pasta (about 75g per person)
Persillade: 30g parsley leaves, blended
with a clove of garlic and 30ml extra
virgin rapeseed oil.
Parmesan

Method:

1.   Blend all the ingredients for the patties in a food processor.
2.   Make a small patty and fry it in a little oil to check the seasoning.
3.   When you are satisfied with the flavour, make the rest of the
      mixture into patties and fry them in batches for 20 minutes, turning regularly.
4.   Cook the pasta in boiling water (with a large pinch of salt) until al dente.
5.   Serve the patties with the pasta, dotted with the persillade, and a few
      shavings of Parmesan.

Bibury Trout Farm
Trout farmers, Gloucestershire

This trout farm in beautiful Bibury was founded in 1902, in order to breed native Brown Trout to supply local rivers. In 1976 the farm stock was wiped out in a drought, and then reopened with rainbow trout, which are more suited to pond conditions.

In the mid 1960s visitors started to come to the trout farm, and it was extremely popular, but numbers have now dropped off somewhat as Sunday opening hours mean that many families choose to go shopping rather than on an excursion to a fish farm! In 1984 they opened their shop, and now they sell both fresh and smoked fish as well as prepared foods such as pâté and fish cakes. In 2001 Kate Marriot and her husband Terry Allen bought the farm. They have done their own smoking since 2009, and Kate kindly gave me some of their smoked trout which is truly delicious.

There are fifteen acres of ponds stretching into the distance, filled with water from the mill stream of the now disused Arlington Mill. Visitors can walk around a third of the area, which has been arranged with flowerbeds, a café and a barbecue area. People can catch their own trout and cook them, or take them home. A surprising amount of wildlife is attracted to the area, such as water voles, heron, kingfishers and otters. In fact, they can be seen as pests, as herons and otters alone take trout to the value of £5,000 a month. Increasingly the focus is on the visitors' side of the business, but they also sell fish for restocking rivers, as well as to a local wholesaler.

The quality of fish is excellent, and it is good to have the opportunity to buy fresh fish at the same time as visiting the farm where they have been reared.

Website Address:
www.biburytroutfarm.co.uk

Phone Number:
01285 740215

Address:
Bibury, Cirencester,
Gloucestershire
GL7 5NL

Opening Times:
See website for seasonal opening times.

Where to Buy:
At the farm shop

Trout en Croûte
with asparagus

Ingredients:

A couple of bunches of asparagus
A little extra virgin rapeseed oil
Sea salt and freshly ground black pepper
Puff pastry (see below)
500g trout fillet in two pieces, skin
removed, trimmed
1-2 tablespoons mayonnaise
50g rocket
1 free-range egg, beaten

Method:

1. Preheat the oven to 200°c, gas 6.
2. Place 6-8 spears of asparagus on a griddle with a little oil and cook until they are lightly coloured. Season well.
3. Cut the puff pastry into two pieces, one slightly larger than the other.
    Roll out the smaller piece of pastry, and place on a lightly oiled baking tray.
4. Season the trout with sea salt and freshly ground black pepper.
5. Place one piece of trout on the smaller piece of puff pastry, then spread it with the mayonnaise. Add the asparagus and most of the rocket. Place the other piece of trout on top (make sure the trout is not too thick: if it is, then gently hammer it, to thin it out, ensuring that it cooks through.)
6. Brush the edges of the pastry with some of the egg.
7. Roll out the second piece of pastry and place over the trout. Seal the edges of the pastry. Make a couple of cuts in the top of the pastry to let the hot air out. Brush with some more of the egg, and chill in the fridge for at least half an hour.
8. Brush with another layer of egg, then bake for 10 - 15 minutes.
    Reduce the heat to 150°c, gas 2, then cook for a further 5 - 10 minutes.
9. Place the trout on a dish. Serve with the rest of the asparagus (griddled in the same way as before) and the remaining rocket.

Rough puff pastry:

Ingredients:

225g plain flour
A pinch sea salt
150g butter, straight from the fridge
Some very cold water

Method:

1. Sieve the flour and salt into a bowl.
2. Cut the butter into smallish pieces and add to the flour.
3. Add enough water to bind the mixture.
4. Roll the pastry into a rectangle, then fold into three. Repeat three times.
5. Put the pastry in a plastic bag and chill in the fridge for at least 20 minutes.

Monument Farm
Beef farmers, Calne

Jean Pocock has been farming at Monument Farm since 1966. It is very much a family business, with a daughter, a daughter-in-law and two grand daughters involved, as well as her sons.

They produce beef (Aberdeen Angus), pork (the pigs are fattened in open straw yards), bacon (cured by themselves), lamb, pheasant, milk and free-range eggs. The abatoir is just up the road, minimising stress to the animals, and they do the butchery themselves.

They make pies that look delicious, as well as pasties and sausage rolls. Jean sells to farmers' markets, two local shops and a local pub, as well as selling from their own farm shop. She has a contract with Waitrose, which makes all the difference to financial survival. Waitrose is committed to supporting local farmers, through their Small Producers' Charter, ensuring 'a fair and ethical relationship' with them.

Website Address: N/A

Phone Number:
01249 740202

Address:
Monument Farm, Bremhill
Calne, Wiltshire. SN11 9LF

Opening Times:
Monday - Friday   9am - 7pm
Saturday   2pm - 6pm

Where to Buy:
Own Farm Shop

Where to Eat:
The Dumb Post Inn, Bremhill, Calne

Newton Farm Beef
Butchery and farm shop, near Bath

Hugh Gay is a third generation tenant farmer on Duchy of Cornwall land in the beautiful village of Newton St Loe. He is developing a pedigree local breed of cattle, the South Devon, ideal because they are naturally large and at the same time mild in temperament. The 'single suckled' calves remain with their mothers for nine months, and then go out into the fields for the summer. In the winter they live in barns where they are fed on silage from grass grown on the land during the summer. No artificial fertilisers or chemicals are used on the land and the farm is part of an environmental scheme called Higher Level Stewardship (HLS). This involves planting trees, native grasses and hedges, as well as restoring ponds and dry stone walls.

Hugh's wife, Celia, runs their Farm Shop, with a butchery section where they sell their excellent dry-aged beef, which is hung for twenty-eight days, as well as other local meat and products. The Farm Shop has been designed using as many recycled materials as possible and has tables where you can sit and enjoy tea or coffee and cakes. They provide the beef for Bistro La Barrique, and Michel, chef and owner, gave a demonstration in the shop of how to cook their rib eye beef. It was heavenly! The quality of their meat received public acclaim when they won Taste of the West Flavour Gold Award in 2012.

Web Site Address:
www.newtonfarmfoods.co.uk

Email address:
hugh@newtonfarmfoods.co.uk

Address:
Newton Farm, Newton St Loe
Bath, BA2 9BT

Opening Times:
Monday - Saturday   7am - 5.30pm
Sunday   10am - 4pm

Where to Buy:
Own farm shop, with deliveries
Prior Park Garden Centre, Bath

Thai Style Beef
with a chilli dipping sauce

Ingredients:

150g fragrant Thai rice (75g per person)
1 large red chilli, de-seeded and chopped
3 teaspoons finely chopped garlic
2 large pinches of sea salt
2 teaspoons sesame or sunflower oil
300g minced beef
100g green beans (roughly chopped)
1 medium-sized red sweet pepper, cut
into strips
3 tablespoons soy sauce
4 tablespoons good stock
1 large splash fish sauce
4 teaspoons golden caster sugar
50g sweet Thai basil

Method:

1. Put the rice into a saucepan and cover with warm water. Stir until most of the starch from the rice has been transferred into the water.
2. Drain the rice and then cover with boiling water and cook until tender.
3. Mix the chilli, garlic and a large pinch of salt in a pestle and mortar or small food processor.
4. Heat the sesame oil in a wok at full temperature until the oil smokes. Add the mix of garlic, chilli and salt, stirring constantly.
5. Once the garlic mix becomes brown, add the beef and stir until cooked.
6. Add the green beans and sweet red pepper. Stir for around 2 minutes.
7. Add the soy sauce, stock, fish sauce and sugar. Stir and heat until close to boiling for approximately 2 more minutes.
8. Finally add the sweet Thai basil. If frozen, add and cook for 2 more minutes; if fresh, add then turn off the heat immediately. Add only the leaves and not the stalks, but don't bother chopping. (If using frozen Thai Basil, do not defrost, as the leaves will become black and unusable – cook straight from the freezer).
9. By this stage the rice should be cooked. Place in a bowl and add the meat.

Note: This recipe was given to me by my son Tom, who is an excellent cook and who loves Thai food. I tend to use less chilli than him!

Chilli Sauce (Hot):

1 red chilli, deseeded and finely chopped
1 green chilli, deseeded and finely chopped
3 tablespoons lemon juice
3 tablespoons fish sauce

Method:

Mix all of the ingredients in a small bowl

Note: Chilli sauce can be added to Thai Style Beef, or used as a dip for foods such as spring rolls.

Standish Park Farm
Cheese maker, Gloucestershire

Jonathan Crump is the tenant farmer of a 300 acre farm in Arlingham, on the edge of the Cotswold escarpment. All of his animals are rare breeds. Beside the Gloucester cows, there are others such as White Park - beautiful white cows with black markings on their noses. There are around 400 Jacob sheep, whose meat is lean, sweet and gamey, rare breed chickens, and Old Spot and Tamworth pigs.

Jonathan's affection for the animals is clear, and many of them have names, such as the bull who is called Henry. Animals have been part of his life from an early age, and he had his first sheep when he was twelve years old on his parents' five acre smallholding. The cattle are fed on hay, which Jonathan grows himself. He feels that this is better than the silage, which he feels can affect the taste of the milk. When he built a new milking parlour three years ago, he built it in the traditional style. His is a low input, low output approach, which is clearly more sustainable than most systems. For example, the water he uses is from a spring that comes straight out of the hillside.

Jonathan has been making cheese for twelve years, and he reintroduced Single Gloucester cheese in the 1970s, as very few people were making it at that time. It had been seen as a 'poor man's cheese', being made with skimmed milk, and maturing quickly. Double Gloucester cheese takes four months to mature, twice as long as the Single Gloucester. His milk is unpasteurised, which ensures better flavour, and he only uses his own cows' milk for his cheeses. Around a quarter of all of Jonathan's products are sold locally, and they have won prizes at agricultural shows and fairs, as have the cows.

Website Address: N/A

Phone Number:
01453 821486

Address:
Orchard House
Standish Park Farm, Oxlynch
Stonehouse, GL10 3DG

Opening Times: N/A

Where to Buy:
Stroud Farmers' Market (first and third Saturday of the month)
Paxton and Whitfield, Bath

Where to Eat:
The Daffodil in Cheltenham

Truffade
An adaptation of a French recipe that uses Contal cheese

Ingredients:

100g streaky bacon, chopped
30g butter
1kg potatoes, peeled and diced finely
Sea salt and freshly ground black pepper
300g Double Gloucester cheese, cut into thin slices

Method:

1. Place the bacon in a large non-stick frying pan and cook in the butter until golden and crispy.
2. Add the potatoes, mix well so that they are coated with the bacon fat and butter, and cook over a very low heat for about 30 minutes, until the potatoes are soft. Season with sea salt and freshly ground black pepper.
3. Scatter the cheese over the potatoes and cover the pan. Cook over a gentle heat, without stirring, until the base is brown and crisp (about 30 minutes).
4. Turn the truffade upside down to serve, so that the crisp base is uppermost.
5. Serve with seasonal sugar snap or mangetout peas.

Besley's Fruit
Organic fruit, Cheddar.

Cliff Besley's parents ran a nursery, so he decided to use his knowledge and experience on a small-scale enterprise, renting an allotment in Wedmore. His initial aim was simply to raise enough money to pay for a holiday in Corfu, but his strawberries were such a success that he now owns a seven acre farm which produces award-winning fruit. The purchase of the land took all of his money, so for four to five years he and his wife lived in a mobile home, gradually building up the business. In 2005 they could finally afford to build a house on their land, and now he says that for the first time he has a winter ahead of him where he can afford both the time and the money for a holiday.

The area is famous for strawberries due to the heavy soil, which produces a rich flavour. For this reason there were over 400 separate growers in the Cheddar Valley in the 1960s. Each had one or two acres, and each could make a living from that small area of land. Now there are only five left.

In 1996 and 1997 Cliff won the title of 'supreme champion' in Draycott Strawberry Fair. Many asked him the secret of his success, but he wisely kept it to himself. Now he sells his fruit in farmers' markets, and any fruit that is unsold is made into jam in his own kitchen.

Cliff specialises in types of strawberries that the supermarkets don't sell, constantly experimenting with new varieties. He knows that people are increasingly interested in the quality of the food that they eat, whereas in the past they did not differentiate between cheap strawberries from abroad, and delicious homegrown varieties. His fruit is sometimes sold as Cheddar Strawberries, and in season (May to October) they can be found in various farmers' markets in the southwest.

Website Address:
www.fresh-n-local.co.uk

Phone Number:
01934 741256

Address:
Merry Fields, Draycott Rd
Cheddar
Somerset
B527 3RU

Opening Times: N/A

Where to Buy:
Bath Farmers' Market
Bristol Farmers' Market
Stroud Farmers' Market
Axbridge Farmers' Market
www.localfooddirect.co.uk
Newton Farm Foods, Newton St Loe

54

Strawberry Brandy Syllabub
with Somerset Cider Brandy

Ingredients:

500g strawberries
90 ml Somerset Cider Brandy
2 tablespoons caster sugar
2 limes
280-300ml double cream

Method:

1. Put most of the strawberries in a bowl with half the cider brandy.
2. Break them into chunks with a fork, or squeeze them with your hands.
3. Grate the zest of one lime, and squeeze the juice from both limes.
4. Whisk the cream until thick. Add half the sugar and the cider brandy and then the lime juice.
5. Rub the rims of four glasses with the lime halves, then dip the rims into the rest of the caster sugar in a shallow bowl.
6. Divide the strawberries between the glasses, and put the cream mixture on top.
7. Decorate with the reserved strawberries, halved, and the lime zest.

Dreamer's Farm
Dairy Farm, Bruton, Somerset

Simon and Kate Oakley bought Dreamer's Farm in 2003. It cost them everything they had, so with a small child and with Kate expecting their next baby, they lived in a tent on the farm until they could afford a mobile home. Finally, after eight years, they were able to move into the new house that they have build for themselves and their four children.

They have 62 acres, with an extra 20 acres of land, which they use as part of friendly agreements with their neighbours. They started with one house cow, but now they have a herd of cows (Hereford and Jersey), sheep (Lamb Lleyn), pigs (Gloucester Old Spot crossed with Landrace), very free-range chickens, some ponies and a grumpy bull called Finn. The animals are rotated around the land, which helps keep disease down, and they produce their own silage and hay for the winter. The animals are kept outside as much of the time as possible, and during any crisp, dry weather in the winter the animals are all sent out into the fresh air. The sheep are lucky, as they have the full run of the farm all year round.

The Jersey cows produce the most wonderful creamy milk, which is left unpasteurised to preserve its full flavour, and Simon and Kate make some of it into cream and yoghurt. The milking parlour is tiny, with space for only two cows at a time, and the cows are given 'nuts' as a treat to keep them happy while they are being milked.

The lambs, in a pen near the house, are fed on the milk from the Jersey cows. Apparently if they are given commercial milk, they die – which gives a strong indication of the health-giving properties of the very special milk produced by the cows of Dreamer's Farm.

All of Simon and Kate's hard work seems to be paying off: the full flavour and the creaminess of the milk make it a treat, and the cream is truly delectable.

Website Address:
www.dreamersfarm.co.uk

Phone Number:
01749 850016

Email address:
sales@dreamersfarm.co.uk

Address:
North Brewham,
Bruton, Somerset
BA10 OJW

Opening Times: N/A

Where to Buy:
Bath Farmers' Market
Local deliveries, by phone, email and collection

Blueberry Swirl
with Jersey cream

Ingredients:

250ml double cream
2 free-range eggs
1 free-range egg yolk
100g caster sugar

For the blueberry purée
250g blueberries
1 tablespoon caster sugar

Method:

1. Whip the cream until it is thick. If you are using Jersey cream you will hardly need to whip it at all.
2. Whisk the eggs and egg yolk with the sugar until it becomes thick and creamy. This takes about 5 minutes with an electric mixer.
3. Add the cream to the egg mixture. You may need to use a hand held whisk to make sure the mixture is smooth.
4. Blend the blueberries with 2 tablespoons of sugar to make a purée. Sieve this into a bowl.
5. Fold the blueberry purée into the cream mixture, leaving swirls.
6. Freeze for 4-6 hours, then serve.

Mumford's Vineyard
Winery and vineyard, Bannerdown, Bath

The name Mumford evolved from Simon de Montfort who is said to have owned the land in 1250. The farm is near two Roman roads, and Margaret Cox found a Roman coin near a vine. This Roman influence is reflected in the label used on the bottles.

Tony and Margaret Cox moved to the area in the early 1980s and bought a house with a six acre field next to it. In 1985 they went on a wine-growing course, and in 1986 they planted a four acre vineyard with 5000 vines. Their best year was 1996, when they produced 10,000 bottles of wine.

They employ local people to help with the harvest (end of September to the end of October), but they do all the pruning themselves, which has to be done in the cold months of the winter, when the vines are dormant.

Mumford's is a winery as well as a vineyard, unlike many who send their grapes to wineries to be made into wine. Their wines tend to be lower in alcohol than in countries like Australia, because they avoid the use of fungicides, which are used to allow the grapes to stay longer on the vines, developing a higher alcohol content.

Groups of people are encouraged to visit the vineyard and to taste the wine. You can buy the wine in single bottles or in cases, and it is cheaper for cash!

Grapes grown: Kerner, Madeleine Angevine, Triomphe d'Alsace and Reichensteiner
Most popular wine: Mumford's rosé.

Website Address:
www.mumfordsvineyard.co.uk

Phone Number:
01225 858367

Email address :
enquiries@mumfordsvineyard.co.uk

Address:
Shockerwick Lane
Bannerdown, Bath, BA1 7LQ

Opening Times:
Phone or email to arrange a visit

Where to Buy:
Direct from the vineyard
Mail order (phone of email for details)

Where to drink:
Same Same But Different, Bath

Pears in Rosé Wine
with aromatic spices

Ingredients:

300ml rosé wine
50g caster sugar
1 star anise
1 blade of mace
10 juniper berries
4 ripe pears (this is also good with
peaches or nectarines)
Fresh double cream, to serve.

Method:

1. Bring the rosé wine to the boil in a saucepan with the sugar, star anise, blade
    of mace and juniper berries, then reduce to a simmer.
2. Peel, core and quarter the pears, then put them into the simmering wine for
    10 minutes with a lid on, turning them over half way through. If the pears are
    unripe, this may take a little longer. Remove them from the pan.
3. Strain the wine, place it back in the saucepan and boil until it is reduced to
    a syrup. Pour this over the pears.

The Square Garden
The Walled Garden at Longleat

Angus Hilleary grew up in the area around Hornisham, but moved into event management in London and Bristol. He managed bars and restaurants, and gradually his love of food and cooking led him to develop an interest in growing food. He and his veterinary wife, Charlotte, are recreating a working kitchen garden in the beautiful four acre walled garden next to Longleat, designed by Capability Brown, and rented from the Marquess of Bath. When they took it over five years ago it was totally overgrown, but gradually they are getting it under control, taking on one acre at a time. They are helped by a few local volunteers such as Fe, who is a chicken and turkey enthusiast, rearing rare chickens like Orpingtons with their glorious plumage. Angus and Charlotte also have some chickens of their own, which lay eggs with rich, dark orange yolks. This colour is due to the fact that they are able to forage for insects, and also the clover they eat, which grows all across the garden. They are also fed produce from the garden, as well as wild foods such as elderberries when in season.

Angus and Charlotte specialise in baby salad leaves, as well as producing fruit, vegetables, flowers and herbs, all grown from seed, according to organic principles. They also press apples from their orchard for apple juice and cider. Later they want to start planting some fruit trees to replace those that originally grew against the walls. Some lead plaques remain, the earliest from 1928, marking where a Doyenne du Comice once stood. They are hoping to encourage sponsors for the new trees, who will be given fruit and juice from the trees in exchange.

They reared twenty local Saddleback piglets, born on Valentine's Day, from two sows. The pigs are allowed to root around in each section of the garden in turn, helping to make it ready for the next crop. The Bath Arms took ten piglets and reared them, producing their own meat for their restaurant, served with locally sourced foods wherever possible. Like Angus, they believe in 'proper food, done well, with local ingredients.'

Angus sells most of his produce to the Bath Arms, but also has a stall outside the pub on Saturdays, which he jokingly calls the Hornisham market. He is also involved in the Frome Farmers' Market, and often exchanges his vegetables for bread and fish. Angus and the other stall-holders all relish the principle of 'co-operation not competition'.

Website Address:
www.thesquaregarden.blogspot.co.uk

Phone Number:
01985 844160

Address:
The Walled garden at Longleat
Hornisham
Warminster
BA12 7NR

Opening Times: N/A

Where to Buy:
a stall outside The Bath Arms on Saturday mornings
Frome Farmers' Market
Somerset Farmers' markets:
www.somersetfarmersmarkets.co.uk

Where to Eat:
The Bath Arms, Hornisham BA12 7LY

Cranachan

with raspberry and vodka sauce

Ingredients:

400g raspberries
50ml vodka
100g caster sugar
40g medium or coarse oats
400ml double cream
2 tablespoons runny honey
2 tablespoons vodka
Zest of 2 unwaxed lemons (if you cannot find unwaxed lemons, you can pour boiling water over them)

Method:

1. Soak the raspberries in the vodka and half the caster sugar for a couple of hours – or longer if possible. Reserve a few of the raspberries then blend the berries and their marinade to a purée.
2. Scatter the oatmeal on a baking sheet then toast it in a low oven, until warm and a little crunchy. Add the sugar and roast for another 5 minutes. (You can also do this in a frying pan).
3. Whip the cream until thick then stir in the honey and lemon zest.
4. Put layers of the cream mixture, the raspberry sauce and the toasted oats in glasses. Top with the reserved raspberries.

Note:
I often set aside some raspberries in a jar with a little sugar, covering them with Vodka. I leave the mixture in the fridge for a few weeks, until the temptation to drink it becomes too great!
This can be sipped as a wonderful accompaniment to puddings.

Autumn

Barbers' Cheddar Cheese
Cheese producers in Somerset

Maryland Farm is set in beautiful countryside, twenty-four miles from Bath. It is a proper family business and although there is a large staff, the family know each of them by name, and there is an obvious sense of involvement and loyalty. The wonderful old beams of the office are completely covered with rosettes and awards, and they claim that we are now 'up there with the French' as far as cheese making is concerned.

The key to the family's success is the dedication and passion they feel for both farming and cheese making. Chris Barber said that 'you have to love it to do it'. There are obviously downsides, like wet weather and long hours, but he said that he has 'tasted a lot of things in life that most people will never see: a kingfisher flying by, an otter swimming in the river, or a new-born deer in the early hours of the morning'. With positivity like that, no wonder the cheese tastes so good!

The Barbers claim to be the oldest surviving Cheddar cheese makers in the country. The current family is the sixth generation to continue the tradition. The family started as tenant farmers, but gradually they bought up a group of small farms, until they eventually had 3000 acres. The area produces good grass, having a high rainfall, so it is perfect for dairy farming.

Cheese cultures are an essential part of the formation of the flavour of a cheese. The Barbers' culture is derived from the unique indigenous bacteria in milk from cows in the South West of England. Until the 1980s everyone used traditional liquid 'pint' cultures in cheese making, but they are delicate and can easily be destroyed, leading to waste. Many turned to the new freeze-dried cultures, which are more resistant, saving money and time. As a result, live cultures became increasingly rare, so the Barbers obtained a range of 'mother cultures', built a laboratory, and have tended the collection with great care ever since. A microbiologist is employed to run the laboratory, and the culture is now used by many artisan cheese makers.

There is a focus on environmental issues such as water recovery and the avoidance of waste. The farm is a centre for the filtering of all Somerset whey through membranes, producing a powder that is used in baby milk formula, and which is also used by body builders. A by-product, lactose, is used as feed for pigs.

Barbers also produce Maryland Farmhouse butter, and some of their Cheddar cheese is also sold under the Maryland label.

Website Address:
www.barbers1833.co.uk

Phone Number:
01749 860666

Email address :
sales@marylandfarm.com

Address:
Maryland Farm, Ditcheat,
Shepton Mallet , BA4 6PR

Opening Times: N/A

Where to Buy:
www.barbers1833.co.uk
www.localfooddirect.co.uk
Chandos Deli, Bath
Nibbles Cheese Shop, Guildhall, Bath

Roasted squash soup
with melting cheese

Ingredients:

1 squash (or pumpkin)
2 tablespoons extra virgin rapeseed oil
A few sprigs of thym
40g butter
1 large onion, chopped
2 cloves of garlic, chopped
10g fresh turmeric, grated, or 1 teaspoon of the powdered form.
500ml good stock
200ml milk
100g Cheddar cheese, diced
50g bread, cut into small cubes
2 tablespoons plain yoghurt

Method:

1. Cut the squash in half and remove the seeds. Brush the cut halves with half of the oil, sprinkle with the thyme, season and put them on a baking sheet. Roast in the oven at 180°c, gas 4, for about an hour, depending on the size.
2. Melt half the butter in a large pan and add the onion. Fry for 15 minutes, then add the garlic and turmeric and fry for a further 5 minutes. Add the stock and milk (you can use different proportions of stock and milk, but a total of 700ml is about right). Add the squash (scooped out of the skin), and season. Simmer for 20 minutes. Lime juice can also be added to sharpen the flavour.
3. Allow the soup to cool, then process the soup to a purée.
4. Pour the soup into a pan, then add the cheese. Stir until it has melted.
5. Heat the rest of the oil and butter in a frying pan, and fry the bread until golden to make the croutons.
6. Pour the soup into bowls, and add a spoonful of yoghurt and some croutons.

Barber's cheese and caraway sablés

Ingredients:
100g Cheddar cheese, grated
100g butter, softened
100g plain flour
1 medium free-range egg yolk
Caraway seeds to garnish

Method:

1. Mix the cheese, butter and flour until a dough is formed. Shape the dough into a roll 4 cm in diameter. Wrap in cling film and chill for an hour.
2. Heat the oven to 190°c. Line 2 baking sheets with baking paper. Slice very thin discs from the chilled dough and arrange on the baking sheets.
3. Brush some egg over the tops of the biscuits. Scatter the caraway seeds on the top. Bake in the oven for 6-8 minutes until golden and slightly puffed up. Cool on wire racks.

Dorset Down Mushrooms
Cultivated mushrooms, Sherborne

George Pointing has been growing mushrooms for over fifty years. He moved to Dorset twenty years ago and in 2001 he and his wife, Nicola, changed their business from the production of white mushrooms for a supermarket, to a smaller-scale operation growing chestnut mushrooms and some exotics such as shitake and oyster.

As their business has grown, Nicola has focused on the business side whilst George, who is the grower, has become the front man at the farmers' markets, where his friendly approach is appreciated by their many regular customers.

Chestnut mushrooms are harder to grow than mainstream crops, and there is not such a high yield, but the taste is better, and there is a longer shelf life. The polytunnels in which they are grown must remain at an even temperature and humidity; a pump that heats or cools the area, creating a microclimate.

George grows his mushrooms in bags, which he believes to be important in order to allow the full flavour and firm texture of the chestnut mushrooms to develop. The bags are left for three weeks to start the growth process of the mycelium. A peat and chalk mix is then placed on top of each bag, and production is staggered in order to maintain continuity in fruiting. There are two female pickers who grade the mushrooms as they go along, thinning out the smaller ones to allow the rest to grow larger and rounder. The biggest ones are the Portabella mushrooms, which can become enormous as well as delicious.

They do not use any pesticides or fertilisers, which is possible in a small-scale enterprise like theirs. Larger producers have to use them to control the invasion of other spores into their crop.

George and Nicola sell their mushrooms at five or six farmers' markets a week, as well as to some forty restaurants and farm shops. They are also involved in the Somerset Farmers Direct box-scheme (www.localfooddirect.co.uk), that has emerged from the farmers' markets, transforming the livelihoods of many small farmers.

George and Nicola won best stall-holders in the Taste of Dorset awards in 2010.

I recommend you to visit them at a farmers' market near you, so that you can enjoy a free taste of their delicious mushrooms, cooked in butter and smelling heavenly!

Website Address:
N / A

Phone Number:
01963 220007

Address:
Dorset Down Mushrooms Ltd
Pointington
Sherborne
Dorset DT9 4LF

Opening Times: N/A

Where to Buy:
Bath Farmer's Market, Green Park Station (Saturday Mornings)
Dick Willows, Bathford
www.localfooddirect.co.uk

Mushrooms with a Crispy Topping
with home-made mayonnaise

Ingredients:

1 tablespoon extra virgin rapeseed oil
1 shallot, chopped
150ml white wine
300g chestnut mushrooms, chopped
50g dill mayonnaise (see below)
25g fresh breadcrumbs
50g grated cheese
1 bunch of flat leaf parsley, leaves
removed and roughly chopped

Method:

1.   Heat the oven to 180°c, gas 4.
2.   Fry the shallot in the oil for 5 minutes.
3.   Add the wine and simmer for 5 minutes, until the volume is reduced.
4.   Add the mushrooms with salt and freshly ground black pepper. Cook gently for about 15 minutes.
5.   Turn off the heat, then add the mayonnaise, and mix well.
6.   Put the mixture into 4 individual ramekins.
7.   Mix the breadcrumbs, cheese and parsley.
8.   Sprinkle this mixture over the mushrooms and bake for 10 minutes.

Dill Mayonnaise

Ingredients:
2 free -range egg yolks
Half a teaspoon sugar
300ml light oil, such as sunflower
1 free-range egg
1 teaspoon of mustard
2 teaspoons of cider vinegar
2 tablespoons fresh dill, roughly chopped

Method:
1. Place the egg yolks in a small food processor. Blend them with the sugar.
2. Add the oil, one drop at a time until you have used up half the oil, blending all the time.
3. Add the egg, mustard and cider vinegar, then the rest of the oil in a thin stream. Continue to blend the mixture. Add the dill and blend, then adjust the seasoning. You may like to add a squeeze of lemon juice.
4. Season well.

Fussels Rapeseed Oil
Producers of extra virgin rapeseed oil

Andy Fussel's family has been farming in Somerset for generations. Many farmers have grown oil seed rape as part of their system of rotation, but five years ago the price dropped dramatically, so he needed to add value to his crop. He did this by introducing a cold-pressing system, so that they could produce a culinary grade of rapeseed oil with a better nutritional value than that produced by hot pressing.

Fussels oil is extra virgin as it is only pressed once, resulting in very low acidity. It has ten times the omega 3 value of olive oil, and half the saturated fats. It is also better to cook with than olive oil, as it maintains its integrity up to higher temperatures.

Fussels oil is used by an increasing number of restaurants and hotels, and the oil that has been used in their deep fryers is collected and returned to Fussels to be processed and then used as biodiesel, fuelling the vehicles used by the company.

Rape meal, the by-product of the pressing process, is used as animal feed, so waste is kept to a minimum.

In 2011 they won a Taste of the West Gold Award, and people are finally realising that we can buy a superb local oil that is as good as any imported olive oil. This means that we can be healthier as well as supporting our local economy and dramatically reducing food miles. I give all those attending my cookery courses a taste of the oil: they are always impressed, as both the flavour and colour are outstanding.

Website Address:
www.fusselsfinefoods.co.uk

Phone Number:
01373 831286

Address:
Church Farm, Rode, Nr Frome
Somerset. BA11 6PW

Where to Buy:
online
Bath Farmers' Market
Dick Willows, Bathford
Goodies Delicatessen, Larkhall
Harvest, Bath
Prior Park Garden Centre, Bath
PJs Farm Stall, Green Park, Bath
Hartleys Farm Shop, Winsley
Newton Farm Shop, Newton St Loe, Bath
www.localfooddirect.co.uk

Pureé of Cavalo Nero
with Parmesan or Pecorino

Ingredients:

230g cavalo nero
4 tablespoons crème fraîche or plain yoghurt
3 tablespoons extra virgin rapeseed oil
3 tablespoons finely grated Parmesan or Pecorino cheese
1 teaspoon whole grain mustard

Method:

1. Strip the cavalo nero from the stalks.
2. Rinse the cavalo nero and then steam it for 12 minutes, or blanch in boiling, salted water.
3. Place the leaves in a food processor adding the crème fraîche, oil and Parmesan by the tablespoonful. Add the mustard, and taste repeatedly. Continue to process until the desired consistency has been achieved.
4. Serve on fingers of toast, rye bread or warm focaccia.

Note:
This recipe comes from my friend Ian Wilson, whose cooking is a great source of pleasure to all those lucky enough to taste it. He varies the recipe, for example by adding anchoves.

Bulgarian Banitsa
with feta cheese

Ingredients:

50 ml extra virgin rapeseed oil
12 sheets of filo pastry, about the same size as the dish you are using (you can cut them so that they fit)
200g feta, crumbled
4 free-range eggs, beaten
100g young spinach leaves, roughly chopped
A pinch of sodium bicarbonate
100 ml plain yoghurt

Method:

1. Use a little of the oil to grease a rectangular ovenproof dish (about 30 x 20 cm).
2. Brush three sheets of the filo pastry with oil and place in the bottom of the dish.
3. Mix the feta with the eggs, spinach, sodium bicarbonate and yoghurt. Spread half of this mixture over the filo pastry.
4. Continue to layer the filo pastry (brushed with oil) with the filling, finishing with 3 layers of filo pastry.
5. Bake oven 180°c, gas 4, until a wooden cocktail stick comes out clean (about 30 – 40 minutes).

Note:
This recipe has been approved by my Bulgarian friend, Mina Bancheva, who is a bountiful provider of delicious meals.

Vincent Castellano's Charcuterie

Charcuterie, Bristol

Vincent Castellano was born in Italy, but did his two-year apprenticeship as a charcutier in France at the age of fourteen. He came to England in 1983 and found that there were no openings in charcuterie at that time, so he trained as a chef and worked in various restaurants, including The Glass Boat in Bristol. However, he was determined to become a pioneer in the rediscovery of charcuterie in this country.

Vincent set up his production unit, or 'laboratoire', in Kingswood, Bristol. He says that charcuterie is like chemistry, involving precision and consistency. The skill lies in the seasoning as well as in the maturation and fermentation processes. Vincent says that this maturation results in a breakdown of fat, so that it is no longer saturated. This makes it healthier than sausage, in the same way as sourdough bread is healthier than ordinary bread, being more digestible.

His favourite way of cooking chorizo is simply to fry it in a little light oil with a persillade (chopped garlic and parsley). He then deglazes the pan with some white wine. I tried it, and it's gorgeous.

When I asked him the difference between cooking chorizo and chorizo that is ready to eat, he answered six weeks: that is how long it takes to mature. 'Fresh' or cooking chorizo is cured but not fully matured and has a relatively short shelf life. 'Ready to eat' chorizo is fully matured and can also be used in cooked dishes, giving a more intense flavour.

Vincent won gold for his pâté de campagne in 2009 and 2011 at the Great Taste Awards. He also won gold stars for his pancetta, dry cured back bacon and Italian coppa in 2010.

He buys his pigs from the high quality abattoir in Ensors, Gloucestershire. Everything these days has to be traceable, so that he can be sure that he is buying free-range animals such as woodland pigs, or Gloucestershire Old Spots. These pigs are ideal for his products, as they are full of flavour.

He regularly trains apprentices, as he believes in the importance of passing on the skills he has perfected.

Website Address:
www.castellanos.co.uk

Phone Number:
0117 9571193

Email Address:
charcuterie@castellanos.co.uk

Address:
Unit 40, Station Road,
Kingswood,
Bristol , BS16 3TE

Opening Times: N / A

Where to Buy:
Order online
Bath Farmers' Market
Bristol Farmers' Market

Chorizo
with halloumi and red peppers

Ingredients:

200g chorizo
150ml cider or wine, depending on what
happens to be open!
2 red peppers
1 red onion, chopped
1 tablespoon extra virgin rapeseed oil
1 clove of garlic, crushed with a teaspoon
of coarse sea salt
1 teaspoon thyme leaves
100g halloumi, cut into cubes

Method:

1. Prick the chorizo and place in a pan with the cider or wine. Bring it to the boil then cover and leave to simmer gently for 15 minutes. Turn off the heat and leave it to cool a little.

2. Bake the peppers whole in the oven at 180°c, gas 6, for 25-30 minutes. Allow to cool a little then peel off the skin and remove the seeds. Chop roughly.

3. Fry the onion in the oil for about 10 minutes until softened. Add the garlic and thyme, and cook for a further 2 minutes.

4. Cut the chorizo into cubes. Add these, with the cider or wine they were cooked in, to the onions. Add the pepper and halloumi and cook gently for 20 minutes.

5. Serve hot with crusty bread.

Moorland Farm
Beef farmers, Axbridge

Axbridge is a very attractive medieval town, and Liz Scott comes from a family with long-standing local connections. Her great-grandfather had a butcher's shop there in the late 1800s. Her grandfather took on the shop until 1954 and her father ran the farm until Liz took over in 1984. In 1996 she opened her farm shop, where she sells her traditionally reared Aberdeen Angus beef, as well as eggs and a few other products. Local people come to the shop for the excellent quality of the meat, which is reliably succulent and reared in stress-free conditions. She uses the same slow growing system that her great-grandfather favoured two hundred years ago, and her cattle can be traced back for generations.

The animals are fed on grass on the Mendip Hills, with 350 acres of farmland to roam. In the winter, when the ground gets too wet, they are brought in and are fed hay and 'forage-based' silage. The cows live a long and happy life and one cow, aged 19 years, recently had a calf. The calves are weaned at nine to ten months and when they are two and a half years old, they are taken to a local abattoir only half an hour away. The meat is hung for two to three weeks, ensuring that it will be tender and delicious. It is butchered and packed on site, so the carbon footprint of the meat is as low as possible.

The farmers' markets have been invaluable outlets for Moorland Farm meat, as for so many other farms. Liz was involved with the Bristol Farmers' Market from its outset (one year after the Bath market started, the first in the country). In the last few years the markets have not done as well as in the past, but her loyal customer base has kept her going. Axbridge is well worth a visit, to see the early Tudor King John's Hunting Lodge and to buy some of Liz's succulent beef.

Website Address:
www.moorlandfarm.co.uk

Phone Number:
01934 733341

Address:
Moorland Farm, Portmeade Drove
Axbridge, Somerset, BS26 2BA

Opening Times:
Monday - Wednesday	9.30am - 1pm
Thursday - Friday	9am - 5pm
Saturday	9am - 2pm

Where to Buy:
Own Farm Shop
Axbridge Farmer's Market (1st Saturday of each month)

Where to Eat:
The Oakhouse, Axbridge

Beef Wellington
with rough puff pastry

Ingredients:

600g fillet steak
1 tablespoon extra virgin rapeseed oil
25g butter
2 shallots, chopped
200g mushrooms, chopped
1 tablespoon thyme leaves
Zest of 1 lemon
2 tablespoons creamed horseradish
1 free-range egg, beaten
Rough puff pastry (see below)

Rough Puff Pastry

Ingredients:

225g plain flour
150g butter, straight from the fridge
A pinch of salt
Some very cold water

Method:

1. Sieve the flour and salt into a cold mixing bowl.
2. Cut the butter into walnut sized pieces and add to the flour.
3. Add just enough water to bind the mixture.
4. Roll the pastry into a rectangle, then fold into three.
5. Repeat three times, then chill thoroughly before using.

Method:

1. Choose a piece of fillet that isn't too thick. You can hammer it gently with a rolling pin if it is more than about 5cm thick, to ensure that it cooks through. Heat a little oil in a frying pan and sear the fillet on all sides until brown. Remove from the pan and leave to cool.
2. In the same pan, melt the butter and the rest of the oil, and fry the shallots for 5 minutes. Add the mushrooms, thyme and lemon zest and cook for about 10 minutes. Season with sea salt and freshly ground black pepper. Blend in a food processor, then leave to cool.
3. Make the pastry (see below) and roll it out into a rectangle.
4. Coat the fillet steak in the creamed horseradish, then the mushroom mixture, and place on one side of the pastry rectangle. Fold the pastry over and trim so that there is enough pastry to turn over round the edges. Brush the edges with the beaten egg, and turn them upwards and over, to make a seal. Make a few cuts in the top of the pastry to let the steam out, and brush with beaten egg. Leave to chill in the fridge for at least half an hour.
5. Heat the oven to 200°c, gas 6. Brush the pastry with more beaten egg, then bake for 30 – 40 minutes.

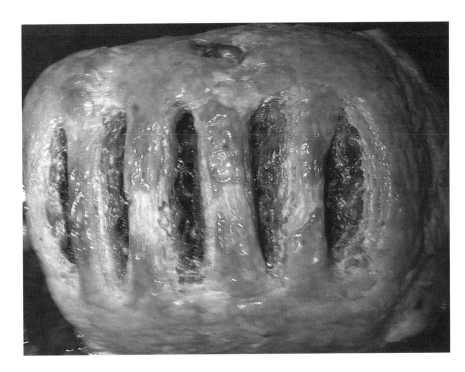

Dartland Farm (Just Chicken)

Free-range chicken farmers, Wiltshire

When Jamie and Emma bought their twenty-seven acres in 2008, the land was without services apart from a water supply. They bought six flat-pack army barracks buildings, which they could use as temporary accommodation for themselves and the chickens until they finally got permission for a permanent farmhouse three years later. The local blacksmith devised a system for the chicken houses so that they could be moved regularly to reduce any negative impact on the land. They have enough land for four times as many birds as they currently keep, but they are keen to avoid intensive rearing. The birds live a comfortable life with branches to climb on, dust baths and hay bales.

They have a very high welfare approach to rearing the chickens, reducing any stress for them as far as possible. The chickens never leave the site, and there is no transport involved, apart from the use of a trailer to move the chicks to the larger chicken houses. Even this is done with a maximum of concern for their well being, and they are moved before daylight, when they are still sleepy. The same applies when they are 'dispatched', which is carried out in the early hours in a little on-site trailer.

Jamie, an ex-chef, is responsible for dry plucking the birds, described as a hand-finished approach. There is no waste, and the giblets are boiled up to make stock for the gravy to accompany his chicken rolls with cranberry sauce and home-made stuffing, which he sells at the farmers' market in Swindon on Sunday mornings.

Recently a group of London chefs and maître ds, who were interested in seeing responsible chicken production in action, visited the farm. This has resulted in their supplying the Ritz with their chickens, which is clearly a triumph.

The high level of care for the birds, as well as the focus on sustainability and connection with the local community, is reassuring for all who believe in a return to traditional values in farming.

Website Address:
www.cluckingmarvellous.co.uk

Phone Number:
07801 032444

Email Address:
cluckingmarvellous@hotmail.com

Address:
Dartland Farm
Malmesbury Road, Leigh
Wiltshire, SN6 6RB

Opening Times: N/A

Where to Buy:
Bath Farmers' Market
Swindon Farmers' Market
Order by email

Chicken in red wine
with Somerset Cider Brandy

Ingredients:

2 tablespoons extra virgin rapeseed oil
50g butter
225g streaky bacon, cut up roughly
2 onions, peeled and roughly chopped
1 large free-range chicken, jointed
3-4 sprigs of thyme and 3 bay leaves
1 bottle of full bodied red wine
4 tablespoons Somerset Cider Brandy
400ml stock
8 shallots, finely sliced
4 cloves of garlic, crushed with 1tsp salt
225g button chestnut mushrooms, sliced

Method:

1. Heat the oil and half the butter in a
   large frying pan. Fry the bacon until
   crisp. Lift out and place in a large
   casserole dish.
2. Add the onions to the frying pan and
   fry until golden – about 20 minutes.
   Lift out and add to the bacon.
3. Add the chicken to the pan, with a little
   more oil if necessary. Cook until
   golden on all sides. Add the chicken
   and herbs to the casserole.
4. Deglaze the frying pan with the wine
   and cider brandy. Stir, then pour it
   over the chicken with the stock.
5. Cover and cook at 140°c, gas 1, for 2
   hours.
6. Fry the shallots gently in the rest of
   the butter for around 10 minutes. Add
   the garlic and mushrooms, and fry for
   10 minutes.
7. Add the mushrooms and shallots to the
   casserole dish and season. Cover
   and cook for a further 15 minutes.

Hazelbury Manor Farm
Organic meat, fruit and vegetables, Box

Hazelbury Manor Farm is set in a truly beautiful environment, alongside the manor house and landscaped gardens. The focus is very much on quality of life for the animals, as well as on creating an environment that feels positively therapeutic. In fact Susan Lacroix is a practicing homeopath as well as a farmer, and she hopes to set up a 'care farm' at some point, working with young people with specific problems such as autism or Asperger's syndrome.

The farm is fully organic, with sheep (Wiltshire Horn, formerly a rare breed), cows (Welsh Black) and pigs (Saddleback). Susan and her husband started with one sow, and built up their stock over the years. Recently they have had to reduce the number of animals they keep, especially the pigs. Saddleback pigs are a rare breed which have a thick layer of fat, enabling them to live outdoors in the woods even in the cold weather,` but these days people prefer to eat leaner meat. There is also a cost issue as the price of grain has risen and organic standards do not permit the use of genetically modified soya, making it hard to keep prices competitive. They now only have three sows, along with sixteen cows with their 'followers' (calves and young stock), and fifty-nine ewes with lambs.

The nearest organic abattoir is in Gloucestershire, which is rather further than Susan would like the animals to travel. Many of the local abattoirs have closed, and attempts to set up a co-operative humane abattoir and organic butchery nearer to home failed due to the cost and burden of EU regulations.

Susan and her husband also grow organic fruit and vegetables in a well-kept kitchen garden, orchard and greenhouses; these are available on request, depending on season and availability.

You can buy Susan's very special meat at Bath Farmers' Market, or you can order by phone or email, and collect it from her. This is well worth doing, as it means that you can enjoy a visit to this spectacular farm.

Website Address: N/A

Phone Number:
01225 812088

Email Address:
slacroix@btinternet.com

Address:
Hazelbury Manor
Box, Corsham
Wiltshire, SN13 8HX.

Opening Times: N/A

Where to Buy:
Bath Farmers' Market (1st and 3rd Saturday of each month)
Order via email or phone
Neston Park Farm Shop, Atworth

Lamb Fillets
with a crispy herb topping

Ingredients:

400 – 600g lamb fillet
1 tablespoon extra virgin rapeseed oil
40g Parmesan cheese, grated
80g fresh breadcrumbs
1 - 2 cloves of garlic, crushed with a little coarse sea salt
40g fresh herbs, such as sorrel, mint or basil, chopped
8 anchovies, chopped, with a teaspoon of the oil from the jar or tin

Method:

1. Trim the fillets of lamb, then flatten them with a rolling pin. Cut them up into 4 individual pieces, about 100 - 150g each.
2. Heat the oil in a frying pan and sear the lamb fillets briefly on both sides. Place them in a lightly oiled ovenproof dish.
3. Combine the cheese, breadcrumbs, garlic, herbs, anchovies and oil. Add some freshly ground black pepper and press this onto the lamb pieces. Cover and place in the fridge for an hour or two.
4. Heat the oven to 180°c, gas 4, and roast the lamb pieces, uncovered, for 20 minutes, until golden and crisp.

The Wiltshire Smokehouse
Sutton Veny, Warminster

Jon Symes produces a range of meat and fish in his traditional smoker near Warminster. He uses oak chippings from a furniture-maker in an adjacent unit, and the chicken he smokes is local, from nearby Melksham. This helps to reduce the carbon footprint of his products.

People can take their own meat along to be smoked, for example pheasant after a shoot, or fish caught by local anglers. They also smoke bacon and hams for people who rear their own pigs locally. Jon likes to make a salad of smoked chicken and mango, with salad leaves and balsamic vinegar.

The smokehouse was awarded bronze and silver medals at the Taste of the West in 2004/5, as well as winning awards for their pork and eel, and in 2011 their smoked Cheddar cheese won a silver medal at the Frome Cheese Show.

They attend ten farmers' markets a month and you can also order online through the website. They are proud to say that they supply the smoked salmon for the catering company that provides meals for the queen's airplane!

Website Address:
www.wilts-smokehouse.co.uk

Phone Number:
01985 840452

Email Address:
jon@wilts-smokehouse.co.uk

Address:
Unit 16, Deverill Road Trading Estate
Sutton Veny, Warminster
BA12 7BZ

Where to Buy:
Farmers's Markets in Wiltshire such as Frome or Bradford on Avon.

Smoked Chicken Salad
with a Thai style dressing

Ingredients:

For the salad:
50g unsalted peanuts or cashews
1 tablespoon extra virgin rapeseed oil
1 onion, peeled and finely chopped
150g thinly shredded cabbage
1 medium carrot, grated
30g coriander, chopped
3 shallots, finely sliced
2 cloves garlic, crushed with a little
coarse sea salt
800g smoked chicken meat, shredded
Half a cucumber, pickled (see below)

For the dressing:
200ml fish sauce
2 tablespoons fresh ginger, finely grated
75ml water
3 cloves garlic
1 red chilli, de-seeded and chopped finely
1 tablespoon sugar
3 tablespoons of fresh lime juice or more
to taste

Method:

1.   To make the salad, heat half the oil in a frying pan, then add the onion. Fry for about 10 minutes until softened. Add the cabbage, carrot and coriander, and place in a large bowl.
2.   Combine all of the ingredients for the dressing, and mix with the salad.
3.   For the topping, fry the shallots in the rest of the oil until golden. Add the garlic and fry for a couple of minutes.
4.   Fry the nuts in a pan (without any oil) until they start to take on some colour. Remove them from the pan and crush with a mortar and pestle.
6.   When you're ready to serve, toss the chicken and pickled cucumber into the salad and mix well.
7.   Scatter the fried shallots and garlic over the salad, then top with the nuts.

Note: This was given to me by my son Tom, who makes this dish regularly. It is quick to prepare and is delicious.

Pickled Cucumber:

Ingredients:

Half a cucumber
⬜ tablespoon sea salt
75ml cider vinegar
2 tablespoons caster sugar

Method:

1.   Peel the cucumber, then cut it in half lengthways. Remove the seeds with a teaspoon and slice the flesh thinly on the diagonal.
2.   Place the cucumber slices in a bowl with the salt and mix well. Set the mixture aside to rest for 30 minutes.
3.   Heat the vinegar and sugar in a non-reactive saucepan and stir until the sugar has dissolved.
4.   Rinse the salt from the cucumber slices, dry them with a paper towel and add to the vinegar mixture. Stir until well combined.

KG Consultants
Apple juice and ciders, Bathford

Keith Goverd produces a diverse range of apple juices, as well as cider and cider vinegar. His lovely old house near Compton Dando is surrounded by sheds and the equipment needed to run his highly efficient business. He has resisted the urge to expand as this would reduce the level of control he has over the quality of the product.

Keith has a great deal of experience in both the scientific and the practical aspects of food production. He has travelled all over the world, working in a range of areas connected to the food industry, and has a broad understanding of many related issues.

He focuses on traditional methods and good manufacturing and management. For example, in an orchard it is important for there to be plants that encourage the variety of insects and birds necessary for pollination as well as aphid control.

As director and chairman of Bath Farmers' Market, he is very involved in ensuring that good practice is observed, and in particular that foods are correctly labeled to show ingredients and provenance.

The healthy qualities of his excellent cider vinegar come from the malic acid, which is not found in ordinary vinegars, and which helps boost the immune system.

Keith has a zero waste policy. All of the pomace, which is the pressed waste from the apples, is used as compost.

His cider is made from 100% apple juice, unlike many others, which are only required to contain 35% apple juice. Keith says that Somerset cider gets its quality from the combination of its tannin element (giving it a mellow, rich taste due to the oxidization process), and its astringency, with a lemony tartness.

Website Address: N/A

Phone Number:
01761 490624

Email Address:
keith@goverd.co.uk

Address: N/A

Opening Times: N/A

Where to Buy:
Bath Farmers' Market
Dick Willows, Bathford

Juicy Apples
with a crunchy topping

Ingredients:

60g butter
60g fresh breadcrumbs
60g Demerara sugar
600g apples, peeled and cored
50g caster sugar
100ml apple juice
150ml double cream, whipped
25g plain dark chocolate, grated

Method:

1. Melt the butter in a pan, and add the breadcrumbs and Demerara sugar. Cook gently until golden brown and crisp.
2. Cook the apples with the sugar and apple juice until it becomes a smooth purée.
3. Place the apples in a dish, then cover with the breadcrumb mixture.
4. When this is cool, cover with whipped cream and top with the grated chocolate.

Note:
This is a simplified version of a Danish dessert called Bondepige med Slør, meaning country girl with a veil, which my mother used to make.

Hartley Farm
Free-range eggs and much more

I first visited Hartley Farm Shop when meeting up with Fred Swift who was delivering some of his delicious honey. I discovered that they sold free-range eggs from the hens that I could see wandering about in the next field.

The Bowles family has been farming since the 19th century, and now three brothers are running neighbouring farms, each specialising in raising different types of animals.

Richard Bowles runs Hartley farm, which is 150 acres of traditional farmland by the village of Winsley. They keep traditional breeds such as Aberdeen Angus and Hereford cattle, outdoor-reared Gloucester Old Spot pigs, and of course their hens. They are proud of their record of animal welfare, and ensure that there is always complete traceability of animals, vital for animal health and food safety. Environmental issues are seen as absolutely necessary for a modern approach to farming, and the shop concentrates on local, seasonal products.

Tom Bowles, Richard's son, has established the farm shop, which opened in 2008, and which sells the produce of their farm, along with other locally sourced foods. Kate Collyns, their market gardener, supplies fruit, vegetables and plants throughout the year. Tom's focus is on quality, locality and sustainability, and his aim is for the shop to be carbon neutral within the next five years.

The café sells a range of delicious cakes, all made with the butter and cream from Ivy House Farm, owned by Tom's uncle Geoff.

The members of staff in the shop are all well informed about the produce, and how to use it. For example Ed, who works on the butchery counter, also works on the farm. The belief is that every customer should have a special experience when they come to the farm shop, and that this will draw them away from the bland, impersonal atmosphere of the supermarkets. Customer feedback is taken very seriously and influences decisions that are made in the running of the shop as well as the products that are made available.

Tom believes that people are starting to return to the strong sense of community that existed in his great-great-grandfather's day, when people bought food that was produced by people they knew. To encourage this, he runs regular 'Meet the Producer' evenings, as well as organising events such as a 'Family Day' at Easter, and a Market at Christmas.

Tom feels that it is important for the farm to have an educational role, so they have had a local children's author to read from his stories about the old days on the farm, as well as organising tractor rides for children as part of teaching them about agriculture. This is an excellent project to visit and to support, as it represents an exemplary approach to farming and the community.

Website Address:
www.hartley-farm.co.uk

Phone Number:
01225 864948

Address:
Winsley
Bradford on Avon
Wiltshire
BA15 2JB

Opening Times:
Monday - Saturday   9am - 5.30pm
Sunday   10am - 2.30pm

Where to Buy:
Hartley Farm shop, Winsley, Bradford-on-Avon

Chocolate Mousse
with home made meringues

Ingredients:

170g good quality plain chocolate
100g butter
3 free-range eggs
30g caster sugar
6 meringues (see below)
100g raspberries (these can be soaked in
vodka and sugar in advance for an adult
version of this recipe)

Method:

1.   Gently melt the chocolate with the butter.
2.   Allow this to cool, then add the egg yolks.
3.   Whisk the egg whites until stiff, then gradually whisk in the sugar.
4.   Fold the egg whites gently into the chocolate mixture.
5.   Break up the meringues and carefully add them to the chocolate mixture.
6.   Put some raspberries in four glasses, then divide the chocolate mixture between them. Top with the remaining raspberries.

Make Your Own Meringues

Ingredients:

150g free-range egg whites
300g caster sugar
2 teaspoons cornflour
1 teaspoon white wine vinegar

Method:

1. Preheat the oven to 130°c, gas ▢ .
2. Place the egg whites in a clean bowl and whisk until soft peaks form.
3. Add the sugar, a spoonful at a time, while whisking continuously.
4. Gently fold in the cornflour and white wine vinegar.
5. Line an ovenproof tray with baking paper and place spoonfuls of the mixture on the tray (this makes 10 to 12 medium sized meringues)
6. Bake in the oven for about an hour, or until crisp but not coloured. Leave the meringues to cool in the oven after it has been turned off.

Bath Organic Group
A community garden in Bath

The Bath Organic Group is set in Victoria Park. They were lucky to be allocated the acre of land at a time when it was at less of a premium. They started with a 'demo plot' or demonstration garden twenty years ago, but gradually the community issues became more important. A core group of people, who have been involved for many years, organise finance as well as issues such as the rotation of crops.

They always need volunteers, who are welcome to come to work in the garden on Tuesday and Saturday mornings. All helpers go away with a bag of seasonal fruit or vegetables. If you are interested in getting involved, the website will give you the information you need. There is always one 'duty person' around to guide the volunteers through the suggested jobs to be done.

There are four beds of vegetables, which are rotated – about the size of four allotments. In addition there is the equivalent of about sixteen allotments of perennial crops such as apples (fifty varieties), pears, grapes, mulberries, plums, raspberries and damsons.

Various projects have been carried out in the garden such as the building of an earth oven. This was organised by Liz Clarke, and it is now a focal point for social occasions. The indoor areas are also important to ensure that the facilities are used in all weathers.

Tim Baines kindly showed us around, and provided a delicious lunch of olive bread and home-made apple juice, with a selection of fresh beans, mulberries, apples and plums that we picked from the garden. We sat in a covered area with low benches running around the perimeter, often used by younger children during school visits. The chickens, a mix of Bantam Plymouth Rocks, are particularly popular, and are kept in a coop built with community funding.

Lottery funding helped to build two ponds, which are crucial in helping to attract more wild creatures to the garden: the greater the variety, the better the natural balance. A colony of slow worms was brought in from the Bath riverside development, which has also added to the diversity of species.

Produce is sold from a small stall in the Bath Farmers Market once a month, with the additional benefit of informing people of the work that is being done, and of attracting more volunteers. It helps to raise funds, as it costs around £2000 a year to run the garden, to purchase manure and poly tunnels, and to create covered areas. This is an exemplary local venture, and worthy of all of our support.

Website Address:
www.bathorganicgroup.org.uk

Phone Number:
01225 866150

Address:
Lower Common West allotments site, next door to the Victoria Park playground and opposite The Hop Pole pub

Opening Times:
Tuesday	10.30am - 1pm
Saturday	10.30am - 1pm

Where to Buy:
Bath Farmers' Market, the first Saturday of each month, from April to December

Plum Clafoutis
with brandy or rum

Clafoutis is a French country dessert from the Limousin region. Clafoutis comes from the word 'clafir' which means 'to fill'. It is traditionally made with the first sweet cherries of the season, which are left unpitted (kernels are said to add extra flavour while baking). An earthenware dish is buttered and then covered with a layer of cherries, stems removed. A batter of eggs, flour, milk, and sugar - sometimes butter or a liqueur are also added - is then poured over the cherries. The consistency of the batter can be thin (like a pancake batter) or thick and cake-like. The assembled dish is then baked in the oven until the batter is puffed, set and browned. Icing sugar is sprinkled over the top and it can be served with ice cream or softly whipped cream. It is best eaten warm.

Ingredients:

6 -8 plums, halved and stoned
2 tablespoons brandy or rum
2 tablespoons caster sugar
3 free-range eggs
70g caster sugar
70g plain flour, sieved
Pinch salt
150ml double cream
1 teaspoon vanilla extract (not essence, which is an artificial flavouring)
2 tablespoons icing sugar, sieved

Method:

1. Arrange half the plums, cut side up, over the base of a buttered ovenproof dish. Pour over the brandy and 2 tablespoons of caster sugar. Leave for at least 30 minutes.
2. Preheat oven to 170°c, gas 3.
3. Beat together the egg yolks and 70g caster sugar until thickened.
4. Add the flour, salt, cream and vanilla. Stir until smooth.
5. Whisk the egg whites and fold into the batter.
6. Pour the batter over the plums, and bake for 15-20 minutes.
7. Remove from the oven and place the remaining plums, cut side down, over the surface of the pudding. Return to the oven for a further 5-10 minutes.
8. Dredge with icing sugar and serve immediately.

Shipton Mill
Producers of organic flour, Gloucestershire

Shipton Mill is based just outside Tetbury, in a beautiful old mill building. They use organic, traditional grains and have built relationships with craft bakers, creating formulations and percentages to produce breads to suit individual needs. Jonathan, of 'Eleven' breads, told me that micro-bakeries are given preferential prices for flour.

The area is not particularly suitable for growing wheat, but spelt is grown, for example at Sharpham Park. Shipton Mill sells organic wholemeal and white spelt flour, as well as a wide range of flours, including rye, but it is important to know what you want in advance as products are not on display. There is a full list of products on their website in the online shop.

They hold excellent courses in bread making at their centre in Frampton on Severn, Gloucestershire, run by Clive Mellum, who is an expert in all things related to bread. The courses are completely free, and you take home a wonderful range of products. You can find more information at: www.shipton-mill.com/the-bakery/baking-great-bread/bread-making-courses.

Website Address:
www.shipton-mill.com

Phone Number:
01666 505050

Email Address:
enquiries@shipton-mill.com

Address:
Long Newnton
Tetbury, Gloucestershire
GL8 8RP

Opening Times:
Monday - Friday   9am - 5.30pm
Saturday mornings

Where to Buy:
Online: Flour Direct Shop
Harvest, Bath

Apricot and Almond Cake
with organic West Country flour

Ingredients:

500g fresh apricots, halved and stoned
250g caster sugar
2 lemons
2 tablespoons honey
125ml water
2 tablespoons Grand Marnier
For the cake:
250g butter, softened
250g caster sugar
4 large free-range eggs, beaten
100g plain flour, sieved
75g ground almonds

Method:

1. Put the apricots, sugar, juice of one lemon, honey and water in a pan and cook gently until tender – about 30 minutes. Add the Grand Marnier (or another liqueur such as Drambuie).
2. Butter a cake tin (about 20-21cm) and dust lightly with flour.
3. Cream the butter and sugar until light in colour. Add the eggs, a little at a time.
4. Purée 100g of the apricot mixture and add to the mixture with the flour, ground almonds and zest and juice of the second lemon. Mix gently, and pour into the cake tin. Bake the cake in the oven at 180°c, gas 4, for 30-40 minutes.
5. Prick the surface of the cake with a skewer and pour the apricot syrup over while the cake is still hot and in its tin. Leave to cool.
6. Slice up the rest of the apricots and spread them over the top of the cake with some shredded lemon zest.

Winter

The Wiltshire Beekeeper
Locally produced honey

Fred Swift has apiaries located all over Wiltshire and for him the key element in successful beekeeping is spending time with the bees, developing a sense of mutual respect. For this reason, he does not use smoke when working with them.

Over the years Fred has acquired a substantial amount of knowledge about beekeeping and is regularly asked to give talks to associations, clubs and schools. He also runs beekeeping courses throughout the year at Whitehall Garden Centre just outside Chippenham. Many people who attend the courses do not intend to keep bees themselves; they are just there to gain more knowledge to support the bees.

Fred's honey is never treated, but simply spun out of the comb then strained. Fred says the best way to eat honey is when it is on the comb, straight from the hive. Bottled honey should always be kept at room temperature to preserve the active properties and when used in cooking, it should only be added at the last minute.

Honey has many benefits for good health including anti-bacterial, anti-fungal and anti-viral properties and it is said to boost the immune system. There is a belief that eating local honey helps to guard against hay fever, and even that it may help to prevent cancer, especially that of the bowel. It is great to know that honey is good for you as well as delicious.

Website Address:
www.thewiltshirebeekeeper.com

Phone Number:
07974 108625

Email Address:
bees@thewiltshirebeekeeper.com

Address: N/A

Opening Times: N/A

Where to Buy:
Hartley Farm Shop, Winsley
The Tollgate, Tollbridge Inn, Holt
PJs Farm Stall, Green Park, Bath
Allington Farm Shop, Chippenham,
Goodies, Larkhall, Bath.
Newton Farm Shop, Newton St Loe
Prior Park Garden Centre, Bath

Pear and Pancetta Salad
with cobnuts and a sweet honey dressing

Ingredients:

100g cobnuts or hazelnuts
200g pancetta or streaky bacon (roughly cut into fairly large pieces)
20g butter
1 tablespoon extra virgin rapeseed oil
4 pears, peeled, cored, quartered
2 teaspoons honey
2 teaspoons cider vinegar
1 teaspoon mustard
Sea salt and freshly ground black pepper
100 - 150g watercress

Method:

1. Heat a frying pan and toast the nuts for 3 minutes, or until golden-brown. Remove from the frying pan.
2. Heat the pancetta in the same frying pan over a medium heat and cook until crisp. Remove and set aside to drain on kitchen paper.
3. Place half the butter and all of the oil in the same frying pan over a low heat. Add the pears and honey. Turn up the heat and cook for around 5 minutes.
4. Add the vinegar and cook for another minute then take the pan off the heat.
5. Arrange the pears and pancetta on top of the watercress on a serving dish, then sprinkle over the hazelnuts or cob nuts.
6. To make the dressing, return the pan with the pear juices to the heat and add the remaining butter, the mustard, salt and freshly ground black pepper. Cook for a few minutes to warm it through. Pour this dressing over the salad.

Felce Foods
Smoked fish, Gloucestershire

Nick Dance took over the fish and smokery business from David Felce a couple of years ago. His wife, Bonny, who does the cooking alongside Mandy, makes delicious fish pâtés and taramasalata, as well as fish cakes and the occasional paella.

They sell a large variety of smoked fish including organic salmon, haddock, cod's roe and mackerel as well as fresh fish such as John Dory and tuna.

Some of the fish is cured by salting or soaking in brine and then it is smoked in a kiln. It is a fairly simple process, piling up the beech wood chips, lighting them, and smoking the fish in the kiln until it is the correct colour and texture. This is where the skill lies, as timing varies depending on temperature and humidity, which can affect the way the wood chips burn and the length of time it takes to smoke the items in the kiln.

Most of the fish is cold smoked, which involves a slow process in which the fish is in the kiln at a temperature of around 60 – 110 °F. The fish is not cooked, but is infused with the smoke and remains moist. Some of the fish, particularly the organic salmon, is hot smoked. A burner is placed in the kiln so the temperature increases to around 180 °F. This produces a smoky flavour, and a firm, flakey texture.

Ben, who is a keen fisherman, assists Nick and together their enthusiasm ensures a high quality range of foods. Their system is traditional, with a hand-made approach, which allows the subtlety of flavour to emerge in their products.

Website Address:
www.felcefoods.co.uk

Phone Numbers:
01454 269078
07974 977575

Email Address:
nick@felcefoods.co.uk

Address and Opening Times:
N/A

Where to Buy:
Farmers' Markets in Bath, Bristol, Stroud and Swindon.
The Tollgate, Tollbridge Inn, Holt.
Online ordering service coming soon

Smoked Mackerel and Trout Pâtés

Smoked Mackerel Pàté

Ingredients:

150g smoked mackerel, skin removed
50g fresh breadcrumbs
20ml vodka
120g ricotta or cream cheese
10g grated, raw horseradish
1 unwaxed lemon, zest and juice

Method:

1. Blend all of the ingredients together and season with sea salt and freshly ground black pepper.
2. Serve with fresh bread or toast.

Smoked Trout Pàté

Ingredients:

100g smoked trout, bones and skin removed
50g natural yoghurt
30g mayonnaise
1 teaspoon harissa (see below)
Zest and juice of half an unwaxed lemon
1 teaspoon sea salt

Method:

1. Blend all of the ingredients together in a food processor. Check the seasoning.
2. Serve with slices of bread or toast.

Harissa

Ingredients:

100g long, fresh red chillies
Half a teaspoon of sea salt
3 heaped teaspoons caraway seeds, ground
3 heaped teaspoons cumin seeds, ground
4 cloves garlic
100g roasted and peeled red pepper
2 teaspoons tomato purée
2 teaspoons red wine vinegar
4 tablespoons extra virgin rapeseed oil
2 level teaspoons smoked paprika

Method:

1. Remove the tops of the chillies, then slice in half lengthways. Lay each chilli on a chopping board, cut-side up, and gently scrape away the seeds with a teaspoon and discard. Be careful not to touch your eyes after doing this!
2. Dry roast the cumin and caraway seeds.
3. Blend all of the ingredients in a food processor.
3. Taste and season, if necessary.

Sandridge Farm
Pig farmers, Chippenham, Wiltshire

Twenty-five years ago Roger and Rosemary Keen started farming pigs and poultry, delivering eggs directly to their customers. However, as increasing numbers of local women started to go out to work, home deliveries were no longer in demand. They decided to diversify and started to cure their own bacon. They were encouraged by Jane Grigson to resurrect traditional Wiltshire products. Roger said that they were 'proud to produce good quality, straightforward Wiltshire products'.

They have an orchard, and the windfalls are fed to the pigs along with the corn that is grown on their own farm and the beer yeast, which is high in vitamin B, from a local brewery. The abattoir is less than a mile from the farm, and the animals are transported there in the farm truck, minimizing trauma.

The area has been famous for its bacon for many years. Calne was a stopping place on the trade route to London for pigs, and those that could go no further were slaughtered and processed there. The Wiltshire cure was innovative in its time: the sheds were packed with cork and ice, lowering the temperature so that brine could be used instead of pure salt to preserve the meat.

Roger and Rosemary smoke the bacon over oak and beech wood chips for two to three days, which gives the bacon its colour as well as its flavour. They said that not all producers use the natural process of smoking, and some meat is actually painted with dye to give it colour. Roger believes in using traditional methods, and does not add water to his bacon. This means that it does not seep fluid when you cook it.

Working in this way is very labour-intensive. The Keens took on the staff - who brought with them a wealth of knowledge - from the Royal Wiltshire bacon factory when it closed down. Labour costs are high, but providing employment is beneficial for the local economy.

We were given some delicious courgette and chocolate cake with a cup of tea, as we sat in their comfortable farm kitchen surrounded by stunning views of the countryside. They are a helpful and friendly couple, clearly hard-working, but willing to give up an hour of their time to talk to us.

Website Address:
www.sandridgefarmhousebacon.co.uk

Phone Number:
01380 850304

Email Address:
info@sandridgefarmhousebacon.co.uk

Address:
Sandridge Farm
Bromham
Chippenham, Wiltshire
SN15 2JL

Opening Times: N/A

Where to Buy:
Bath Farmers' Market
Frome Farmers' Market
Larkhall Butchers, Bath

Spaghetti Carbonara
with smoked bacon

Ingredients:

25g butter
100g smoked bacon, diced
1 garlic clove, crushed or finely chopped
350g spaghetti or bucatini (allow 75-100g per person)
10g sea salt for every 100g pasta used
4 free-range eggs yolks
80g Parmesan or strong Cheddar cheese, finely grated

Method:

1. Melt the butter in a large frying pan and add the bacon. Fry until golden, then add the garlic.

2. Cook the spaghetti in a large pan of boiling water. Once it has returned to the boil, put on a lid. After 5 minutes remove the lid and stir from time to time, ensuring that it does not stick. Cook until al dente (firm to the bite), then drain, reserving a little of the cooking fluid. Add to the bacon and garlic, using the reserved fluid to 'let down' or loosen the mixture.

3. Remove the pan from the heat, then pour in the egg yolks and half the Parmesan or Cheddar cheese. Season with sea salt and freshly ground black pepper.
    Mix well, so that the egg mixture coats the pasta but does not cook.

4. Add the remaining Parmesan or Cheddar cheese, mix well and serve with some watercress or salad leaves tossed in a little vinaigrette.

Bath Soft Cheese
Cheese producers, near Bath

Bath Soft Cheese company is based three and a half miles from Bath, and is a truly authentic local product. It is made to an ancient recipe, and was mentioned in a letter written in 1801 by Lord Nelson. Graham Padfield's family has been making cheese on the farm for three generations.

He demonstrated his technique for making his famous soft cheese at the Cheese Festival in Milsom Place, Bath in 2011. He adds a pinch of mould or starter to the milk with a pinch of rennet, which he leaves in a warm place to set. He then passes a knife through it to break the bonds of the protein matrix and stirs it so that the liquid or whey is released, leaving the curds or solid element. This is poured into the cheese moulds, allowing the whey to drain out. Salt (2%) is added the next day. After nine days a white mould forms over the outside of the cheese. As the cheese matures it softens from the outside inwards, and the flavour deepens over four to six weeks.

To make his blue cheese, Graham takes salted white curd and breaks it into walnut-sized pieces. This is pressed down in a cheese mould, creating cavities inside, but a smooth exterior. The blue mould needs air to form, so after six weeks, needles are inserted into the cheese so that the mould can breathe. Blue cheese has a life of eight weeks.

To make his hard cheese, Graham uses a basket lined with cheesecloth. He pours in curd that has been heated and stirred. This is then 'dunked' in brine for a day and a half, and it will then last over a year. This cheese has been named The Wyfe of Bath, because it is nice to hold! It has won awards both nationally and locally.

Website Address:
www.parkfarm.co.uk

Phone Number:
01225 331601

Address:
Park Farm, Kelston, Bath, BA1 9AG

Opening Times:
Monday - Saturday   8.30am - 6.0pm
Sunday   10.30am - 4.30pm

Where to Buy:
Bath Farmer's Market
Neston Park Farm Shop, Atworth
Newton Farm Shop, Newton St Lo
PJs Farm Stall, Green Park, Bath
Prior Park Garden Centre, Bath
Newton Farm Shop, Newton St Loe

Baked Cheese in Puff Pastry

with a sweet chilli sauce

Sweet Chilli Sauce

Ingredients
60g caster sugar
3 cloves of garlic, peeled
3 cm piece of ginger, peeled and grated
2 red chillies, de-seeded and chopped
1 large lime
1 teaspoon fish sauce
1 tablespoon light soy sauce

Method:

1. Place the sugar in a small heavy-based saucepan with 4 tablespoons of water. Stir to dissolve the sugar, then bring to the boil for 5-8 minutes until reduced and thickened, and a light caramel colour.
2. Blend the garlic, ginger, chillies and lime juice in a food processor.
3. Add the paste to the sugar syrup in the pan and then stir in the fish sauce and soy sauce. Simmer for 1-2 minutes.

Baked cheese in puff pastry

Ingredients:

250g puff pastry, straight from the fridge
4 teaspoons sweet chilli sauce (see above)
1 whole Bath Soft Cheese (300g), straight from the fridge.
1 free-range egg, beaten

Method:

1. Cut the pastry into two parts, one slightly larger than the other.
2. Roll out the pastry into two squares.
3. Spread half the chilli sauce in the centre of the smaller square.
4. Cut a couple of slits in the top of the cheese and place on top of the chilli sauce. Spread more chilli sauce on top of the cheese, then brush the edges of the pastry with egg.
5. Cover with the larger piece of pastry, folding the edges upwards. Seal carefully to avoid melted cheese from leaking out during cooking. Make a couple of small cuts in the top of the pastry, to let out any steam.
6. Brush the top of the pastry with beaten egg, then put on a flat baking dish. Place this in the fridge for at least half an hour.
7. Preheat the oven at 200°c, gas 6..
8. Brush the pastry with another layer of egg. Bake for 15 minutes until golden. This is a shared first course, but you can make individual 'pies' if you prefer.

Marshfield Organic Farm
Farmers near Bath

Dawn Brooks and Louis Tiley both come from farming backgrounds and started this venture in 1994. BSE had devastated the lives and businesses of many farmers, and as a result DEFRA (the Department for Environment, Food and Rural Affairs) was very active in assisting new farming projects. They spent three days with Dawn and Louis, working out a business plan and with the EU funding that was available at the time they built the butchery that would enable them to sell their meat as organic. The farm was certified organic in 1996, with all calves having to be conceived on organic land.

The Bath Farmers' Market opened in September 1997, and as Dawn already had experience in running the Wiltshire Farmers' Market, she knew that this would be the perfect outlet for their beef. As their reputation grew, people asked for different kinds of meat, and they responded by expanding into lamb, pork and poultry. Eventually they were rearing roughly equal numbers of all of these animals, keeping the numbers relatively small. All of the animals are fed on home-grown organic forage, with access to open pasture. They focused on traditional British breeds: Angus-Hereford for beef, Dorset-Jacob for lamb, and the pork is British Saddleback-Tamworth. The animals are all free- range and live in ideal conditions, so the meat is of very high quality.

We had a walk around the fields next to the farmhouse where we found Mary the sow, with her seven piglets. They were beautiful, some black and some golden, the perfect image of contented livestock. Here, as over the whole farm, there is an emphasis on the natural rearing of young animals by the mother, which clearly helps to maintain a stress-free environment. As a result the animals are healthier and happier.

The poultry also have an exemplary environment, with a range of houses and places to shelter. The 'table birds' are a slow growing breed, and are allowed five to eight months of this comfortable life before they are sold. This is not only a very humane way to raise the birds, but it also greatly enhances the flavour. The birds are hatched from eggs on the farm, and they can grow as large as 6 kg – fed on home-grown organic food, and without the use of any growth promoters.

The farm is very much part of the local community, and young people regularly come for work experience at Marshfield Farm – often at shearing time. They absolutely love it, and always want to stay on. Dawn and Louis do most of the work themselves, with the help of Dawn's father and their son-in-law. The animals live their lives on this lovely farm, and are then sent to a local family-run abattoir near Dursley, ensuring that they undergo a minimum of stress. The older animals, who have names like Buttercup and Old Angus, are allowed to live out their days in peace in the lush green fields that have been their home.

Website Address:
www.marshfieldprganicfarm.co.uk

Phone Numbers:
01225 891397
07920 104211

Email Address:
info@marshfieldorganicfarm.com

Address:
Field Farm, Aylford Lane, Marshfield,
South Gloucester, SN14 8AB

Opening Times: N/A

Where to Buy:
Bath Farmers' Market

Italian-style Beef Casserole
with red wine or port

Ingredients:

50g tin of anchovies
500 - 600g stewing beef, with most of
the fat removed and roughly chopped
2 tablespoons flour with sea salt and
freshly ground black pepper
1 red onion or 2 shallots, chopped
3 cloves of garlic, chopped
300ml stock
100ml red wine or port
70g redcurrant jelly
10g capers, rinsed and chopped
100g artichoke hearts, quartered (I like
the chargrilled ones in oil)

Method:

1. Preheat the oven to 140°c, gas1. Tip half the oil from the tin of anchovies into a frying pan, and place over a medium flame.
2. Dip the beef into seasoned flour, and fry in the oil until well browned. Transfer to a casserole dish.
3. Heat the rest of the anchovy oil in the frying pan. Add the onion or shallots, and fry until softened. Add the garlic and fry for a couple of minutes, then transfer this to the casserole dish with the beef.
4. Add the stock, wine or port, redcurrant jelly, chopped anchovies, capers and artichoke hearts.
5. Bake, covered, in the oven at 140°c, gas1 for two hours.

West Country Game and Deer Park

Deer farm, near Chippenham, Wiltshire

Russell, Johnny and Sam, three school friends from Hullavington, have taken on the deer farm at Woodbarn Farm. Until 2008 it was run by 'three old boys with hearts of gold', and they are still invaluable in the advice they provide. The dairy farmer from whom they rent the farm also gives them help and advice; it seems that everyone is delighted with the energy and enthusiasm that is being poured into the business.

The three friends have learned to deal with the many tasks involved in running the deer farm. Everything is done on site, from rearing the deer, to slaughtering and butchering.

It was expensive to set up the business, but after only three years they were in profit. This is unusual in times of economic uncertainty, but the energy and flexibility that these three young men show demonstrates what can be achieved. Their perseverance has certainly been rewarded, as they now provide game for several top London restaurants. In fact 90% of their customers are restaurants, especially in the Cotswolds, but they also sell at Bath Farmers' Market, which is where I first came across their delicious venison.

80% of their venison is wild, and they have a 'small army of stalkers' who bring in the deer. There are also pheasant shoots, and you can buy partridge, duck, pigeon and rabbit when in season. The venison season runs from September to February.

Apparently game is growing in popularity, and people are becoming aware of the health benefits of eating venison: it is high in protein and iron and low in saturated fats, as well as being a good source of vitamin B12.

I asked Russell his favorite cut of venison and he said the loin. He said that you can fry it for three minutes on each side, and it is perfect. It doesn't need to be marinated as it is very tender. The secret is in the length of time it is hung – red deer are hung for two to three weeks, wild deer for only a week to ten days. My recipe is also simple, with a chutney using seasonal pears.

Website Address:
www.westcountrygame.com

Phone Number:
01666 837524

Email Address:
info@westcountrygame.com

Address:
Woodbarn Farm
Stanton St Quintin
Chippenham, SN14 6DJ

Opening Times:
Wednesday - Saturday   10am - 6pm

Where to Buy:
Online
Bath Farmers' Market (2nd and 4th Saturday of each month)
Gloucester Farmers' Market every Friday

Venison in a port glaze

with pear chutney

Ingredients:

Coarse sea salt and coarsley ground black pepper
4 x 150g pieces of venison fillet, trimmed
1 tablespoon extra virgin rapeseed oil
2 tablespoons port
1 tablespoon redcurrant jelly
Pear chutney (below)

Method:

1. Place the sea salt and black pepper on a plate, and dip the venison into it to season all around the outside of the pieces of meat.
2. Heat a frying pan with a little oil, and fry the venison until browned on one side. Add the port and redcurrant jelly, and shake the pan to distribute the juices. Turn over the venison and fry for a couple of minutes. Remove from the pan and leave to rest for a few minutes.
3. Add the juices to the pear chutney (below) and pour over the venison.

Pear Chutney:

Ingredients:
2 pears, peeled and sliced
2 teaspoons extra virgin rapeseed oil
Half a lemon
1 tablespoon honey
1 teaspoon mustard
1 teaspoon grated ginger

Method:

1. Fry the pears in the oil for 5 minutes.
2. Add the lemon juice, honey, mustard and ginger and cook until it begins to caramelise. It is now ready to eat.

Dick Willow

Cider maker, Bathford

Somerset has a long tradition of cider making, as both soil and climate are well suited to growing apples. When Richard Hudson bought a piece of land outside Bath in 1994, he researched the local crops and conditions and decided to plant an orchard. After six years he was growing nine different types of apple and was making traditional craft cider.

Richard told me that cider 'ferments itself if you keep good practice'. The sugar in the apples is converted to alcohol in the fermentation process, which takes between one and six months, depending on the temperature. It can then be kept in a vat for years, in the right conditions. The apples are pressed on site: the art is in the blending, achieving a balance of sharpness, sweetness and the softness of taste that is distinctive to West Country cider.

Richard and Bella stock a range of excellent local produce in their farm shop, with as much as possible that is organic and free-range. You can sample some of the cheeses, and of course the cider, and there is an onsite café. The aim is to have as low a carbon footprint as possible, and to reduce food miles. They want to encourage people to enjoy making their own food, and to provide an alternative to supermarket shopping.

Website Address:
www.dickwillows.com

Phone Number:
01225 859780

Email Address:
info@dickwillows.com

Address:
Box Road
Bathford, BA1 7LR

Opening Times:
| Monday - Saturday | 9am - 6pm |
| Sunday | 11am - 5pm |

Where to Buy:
Dick Willows, Bathford

Guinea Fowl in Cider

with guinea fowl from Bath Farmers' Market

Ingredients:

1 guinea fowl
Sea salt and freshly ground balck pepper
100ml stock (made with the guinea
fowl carcass, carrots, celery, onions and
herbs)
50g butter
300ml cider
2 apples, peeled, cored and roughly
chopped
1 teaspoon mustard
1 tablespoon Somerset Cider Brandy

Method:

1. Joint the guinea fowl, and set aside the breast, legs and wing joints. Season.
2. To make the stock, boil the carcass in water with the vegetables and herbs. After about 45 minutes, strain the liquid into a jug. Use some in this dish, and keep the rest in the fridge for use in soups and sauces.
3. Melt half the butter in a frying pan and brown the guinea fowl joints.
4. Place in a casserole dish and pour over the cider. Cover and cook in the oven at 180°c, gas mark 4, for an hour.
5. Melt the rest of the butter in the same frying pan that you used for the guinea fowl joints and add the apples. Pour over the stock and cook for a further 30 minutes until reduced.
6. Add this to the guinea fowl with the mustard and Somerset Cider Brandy. Cover and return to the oven for 30 minutes. Check the seasoning and serve.

Bush Farm Bison Centre
Bison Farm and visitor's centre in Wiltshire

Colin Seaford was the first person in the UK to keep bison, although cave paintings show that they were common in this country in prehistoric times. He initially bought four animals, and then decided to start the British Bison Association, described as 'a group of enthusiastic people who keep bison for pleasure or for gain.' The idea is to encourage co-operation and communication among those dealing with bison.

Bison are classed as wild animals so are difficult to herd and dislike being handled. Despite this they are docile in general, and most of the time deer fencing is adequate (Bush Farm was previously used to rear deer). However, when they need treatment, such as their regular copper injections, sturdy crash barriers are needed to contain them. It is important to avoid any contact with sheep, which may carry MCF (malignant catarrhal fever, as this is deadly for bison.)

There is a relaxed atmosphere around the 130 acre farm in West Knoyle, and the animals seem contented. The breeding stock are given names, such as the bull called Mountain William and his 'wives' who are named after the wives of American presidents. The animals are fed grass all summer, with hay and silage in the winter months when they have to be kept in the yard to protect the pasture.

Pepe, Colin's wife, told me that the meat is far more tender than beef. It is low in fat and cholesterol, as well as being high in protein and low in calories, so it is healthier than beef.

Pepe is very enthusiastic about their unusual herd, and about cooking the meat. She makes bison chilli, pâté and pies, which she sells in their shop. She told me that bison meat should be cooked at a lower temperature than beef, and it cooks quickly, so it is important to avoid overcooking. It is best eaten rare. They won an award in 2011 from the Guild of Fine Food for their bison steak and burgers.

They encourage visitors during the summer (the season runs from April to the end of September). The centre is ideal for families who can go on the farm walk, as well as exploring their thirty acres of woodland. There is plenty of wildlife to see as well as the bison and elk that are reared on the farm.

Website Address:
www.bisonfarm.co.uk

Phone Number:
01747 830263

Email Address:
info@bisonfarm.co.uk

Address:
West Knoyle
Warminster, Wiltshire
BA12 6AE

Opening Times:
Wednesday to Sunday

Where to Buy:
Own shop
Salisbury and Frome Farmers' Markets

Bison Meatballs
with a red wine sauce

Ingredients:

For the meatballs:
500g minced bison meat
50g fresh breadcrumbs
Sea salt and freshly ground black pepper
75g mozzarella
3 tablespoons extra virgin rapeseed oil

For the sauce:
2 shallots, chopped
4 teaspoons tomato purée
Juice and zest of 2 oranges
100ml red wine

Method:

1. For the meatballs, mix the minced bison meat with the breadcrumbs and seasoning.
2. Mix well and make about 15 balls.
3. Cut the mozzarella into about 15 chunks.
4. Flatten each meatball and press a piece of mozzarella into the centre. Gather the meat around it and pinch to make sure it is sealed.
5. Heat half the oil in a large frying pan and sauté the meatballs for around 20 minutes until browned, turning occasionally.
6. For the sauce, fry the shallot in the remaining oil until softened.
7. Add the tomato purée, orange juice and zest, and the wine.
8. Simmer for about 5 minutes.
9. Blend the sauce in a food processor if you like it smooth.
10. Serve the meatballs on a bed of sauce.

Ivy House Farm
Dairy farmers, Beckington, near Bath

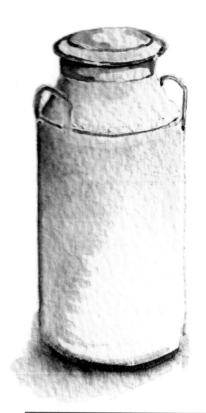

Geoff Bowles started farming at Ivy House Farm in Beckington in 1982, and after a few years he bought a small herd of Jersey cows. At first he sold the milk, butter and cream to Harrods and Selfridges in London, but when he found that there was a local demand for his products he started to sell to the surrounding community. He developed a sustainable approach to farming, using traditional methods alongside the Countryside Stewardship Scheme (CSS) replacing hedgerows and ponds and encouraging wildlife and wild flowers.

In 2012 children from the local primary school visited the farm as part of a project to look at a year on the farm, and this included adopting a calf. This helps the children to understand local food production and farming, teaching them to make better choices in both their eating habits and in creating a sustainable lifestyle. This is farming at its best, combining social awareness and responsibility with a truly excellent product.

Website Address:
www. ivyhousefarmdairy.co.uk

Phone Number:
01373 830957

Address:
Beckington, BA11 6TF

Opening Times: N/A

Where to Buy:
Hartley Farm Shop, Winsley
Dick Willows, Bathford
Prior Park Garden Centre, Bath
PJs Farm Stall, Green Park, Bath
Harvest, Bath
Neston Park Farm Shop, Atworth
Newton Farm Shop, Newton St Loe, Bath
Eades greengrocers, Bath

Where to Eat:
The Long Arms, South Wraxall

Diplomat Pudding
with Somerset Cider Brandy

Ingredients:

120g sultanas
60ml Somerset Cider Brandy
50g melted butter
200g brioche loaf (about 8 slices)
250ml full cream milk
250ml double cream
1 vanilla pod
4 free-range eggs
100g caster sugar
40g Demerara sugar
Extra cream to serve

Method:

1.   Soak the sultanas in the Somerset Cider Brandy for about half an hour.
2.   Preheat the oven to 170°c, gas 3.
3.   Use some of the melted butter to grease an ovenproof dish (about 20cm by 30cm)
4.   Slice the brioche and brush with the rest of the butter. Put the slices on a baking tray and toast them in the oven for 10 minutes until they are golden.
5.   Gently warm the milk and cream with the vanilla pod in a pan until it nearly comes to the boil. Remove from the heat and set aside the vanilla pod.
6.   In a bowl, whisk the eggs and caster sugar until thick and creamy. Gradually pour in the milk and cream mixture. Scrape the seeds from the vanilla pod and add them to this egg custard.
7.   Put a layer of brioche slices into the ovenproof dish, then cover with the sultanas. Top with the rest of the brioche slices.
8.   Pour over the egg custard and sprinkle the top with some Demerara sugar. Make sure that the final layer of brioche is well soaked with egg mixture so that it produces a nice golden colour when baked. Bake in the oven for about 30 minutes. Serve with cream.

Wyle Valley Vineyard
Wine makers, Warminster

In 1989 Paul Dale planted a vineyard with his father, having taken a commercial wine making course at agricultural college, as well as working in vineyards in the UK and in Galicia in Spain.

The site is surrounded by hills and trees so it is ideal for growing vines. He grows Regner, Kernling and Seyval Banc, and his wines are all single grape varieties. He is a small producer averaging 15,000 bottles a year, qualifying as a 'boutique' vineyard. In good years he sells his wine to local farm shops, pubs and restaurants as well as in his farm shop, which he opened in December 2008. He tries to keep his prices down to compete with supermarkets and stocks a good range of locally produced foods. He has good relationships with other local producers, and recommended several people to me.

Paul believes that changes in climate, combined with new disease-resistant strains of grape, mean that in the future the UK will become a major wine-producing country. In fact English wines are already starting to be taken more seriously.

Paul is a resourceful person and 2011's abundant apple harvest encouraged him to use his grape press for making cider. He is involved in a friendly competition with local brewer Chaz Hobden, and market gardener Angus Hilleary of the Square Garden at Longleat.

Website Address:
www.ukvines.co.uk/vineyards/wylye

Phone Number:
01985 211337

Address:
Mill Farm House
Hill Deverill, Warminster
BA12 8BQ

Opening Times:
Monday - Saturday   10am - 5.30pm

Where to Buy:
Their own Farm Shop

Rhubarb Flummery
with white wine

Ingredients:

450ml white wine
Juice of 1 lemon
100g sugar
1 stick of cinnamon
1 kilo rhubarb, roughly chopped
25g butter
Zest and juice of a lemon
25g plain flour
2 free-range eggs
Thick cream to serve

Method:

1. Put the wine, lemon juice, sugar and cinnamon in a pan and heat gently to dissolve the sugar. Then bring to the boil.
2. Drop the rhubarb into the boiling liquid and simmer for 15 minutes. Strain off the syrup, reserving it in a jug and leave it to cool.
3. Pour 250ml of the syrup into a pan with the butter and lemon juice and zest.
4. Mix a further 50ml of the syrup with the flour. Add the egg yolks and mix to a smooth paste. Add this paste to the syrup, butter and lemon juice in the pan and stir over a gentle heat so that it thickens. Cook for about 5 minutes then strain this through a sieve into a bowl.
5. Whisk the egg whites until stiff and fold into the flummery. Fold in the rhubarb, and serve with thick cream.

Somerset Cider Brandy and Burrow Hill Cider
Cider makers, Martock, Somerset

Burrow Hill, at the centre of one of the three main apple growing areas of the country, has been producing cider for over 150 years. There are 160 acres of orchards, in which forty varieties of apple are grown.

Most 'industrial' ciders are 35% apples, and 65% glucose syrup. Farm cider, on the other hand, contains 100% apples. Julian Temperley blends varieties of the fruit tocreate character and to achieve the correct balance of acidity and alkalinity.

At Burrow Hill they press 1000 tons of apples a year. The cider produced is later distilled to make their excellent cider brandy. In 1989 it was given the first ever cider-distilling license in recorded history and the Somerset Cider Brandy Company has also been elected to the City guild of the Worshipful Company of Distillers.

In 2011 Somerset Cider Brandy was finally given 'Protected Geographical Indication', a status that had been opposed by those in Brussels who wanted to keep the term 'brandy' exclusive to a product made with grapes. To celebrate the victory, Damien Hirst designed a box and label for the twenty-year-old brandy. He is a friend of Julian Temperley's daughter, Alice, who is a fashion designer.

It is fascinating to visit the shop, which is an ancient barn full of eccentric equipment (and people!), and you can walk round the orchards where sheep and horses are grazing.

There are tours on offer, with a tremendous amount of information available. When we went there was a group of young men enjoying generous tastings of the excellent range of cider, perry and cider brandy.

I now use Somerset Cider Brandy in all of my recipes, instead of any other kind of brandy. It has an exquisite flavour, and has been compared to Calvados.

Website Address:
www.ciderbrandy.co.uk

Phone Number:
01460 240782

Address:
Pass Vale Farm,
Burrow Hill, Kingsbury Episcopi
Martock, Somerset, TA12 6BU

Opening Times:
Monday - Saturday   9am - 5.30pm

Where to Buy:
Farm shop
Online: www.ciderbrandy.co.uk/shop
Dick Willows, Bathford
Tasting Room, Bath
Prior Park Garden Centre, Bath

Apple Semifredo
with Somerset Cider Brandy sauce

Ingredients:

300g cooking apples, peeled, cored and roughly chopped
Zest and juice of 1 lemon
80g caster sugar
3 - 4 free-range egg whites (depending on size)

For the caramelised apple sauce:
150g caster sugar
2 eating apples, peeled, cored and finely chopped
50 ml Somerset Cider Brandy

Method:

1. Cook the apples in a saucepan with the lemon zest and juice, and half the sugar, stirring occasionally until the apples become a purée. Leave to cool.
2. Whisk the egg whites until stiff, then add the rest of the sugar and continue to whisk for a couple of minutes.
3. Gently mix the apple purée with the egg whites.
4. Line a loaf tin with cling film, then pour in the apple mixture. Fold the cling ilm over the top and put in the freezer for at least 4 hours.
5. To make the caramel, gently dissolve the sugar in a heavy-based pan until it starts to become liquid and to turn brown. Add the apple and stir. Pour in the cider brandy, stirring to dissolve the caramelised lumps that will have formed.
6. To serve, lift the apple semifredo out of the tin and unwrap it. Slice it up and spoon hot cider brandy sauce around these slices. Serve immediately.

Burcott Mill

A working flour mill in Somerset

Burcott Mill is a Victorian watermill whose origins date back to 1864. Steve and Louise took it on in October 2009. The previous owner helped to ease them into the new life that they had taken on, advising them on the use of the complex machinery. They had dreamed of running a guest house together, and the Mill offered so much more.

The mill has had a long and convoluted history. It dates back to the Domesday Book, over a thousand years ago, when it was built for the Bishop of Wells. It has been through phases of productivity and other periods when it has lain idle. It now has many visitors as it is a working museum as well as one of the few examples of a working watermill in the country.

Somerset is not ideal for growing wheat as it is too wet, but spelt has a double husk that protects it. At Burcott Mill they sell organically grown Spelt grain from Sharpham Park, near Glastonbury.

Burcott Mill is the only Soil Association accredited organic, traditionally milled, stone-ground flour in Somerset. Steve and Louise produce three grades of wholemeal flour made from English wheat, which is sold very locally to farm shops, local caterers and customers who come to visit the Mill. They bake their own bread, which is sold from the small post office within the Mill buildings, as well as feeding guests who stay in their guesthouse.

Steve and Louise have a young family, but despite the rigours of parenthood and the work involved in running the guesthouse, their plans for the Mill are constantly evolving. They are interested in using the power of the water wheel to produce electricity, and they want to build a turbine when their finances allow them to do so. They are also interested in linking a cider press to the Mill, using apples from their own small orchard. They relish being part of the local community, and the exciting trend towards working locally to make a difference.

Website Address:
www.burcottmill.com

Phone Number:
01749 673118

Email Address:
enquiries@burcottmill.com

Address:
Wookey Rd, Burcott
Wells
Somerset, BA5 1NJ

Opening Times:
Weekends - Easter to September

Where to Buy:
Their own shop
www.localfooddirect.co.uk
Farm shops in Somerset

Pear and Ginger Pudding
with fresh stem ginger

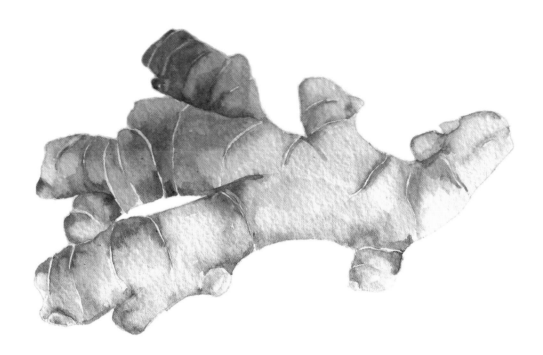

Ingredients:

80g butter
80g Demerara sugar
4 pears, peeled, cored and sliced
2 free-range eggs
120g stem ginger in syrup, sliced finely
3 tablespoons of the syrup from the jar
Half a teaspoon bicarbonate of soda,
dissolved in half a tablespoon water
20g self-raising flour
100g breadcrumbs

For the toffee sauce:
4 pears, peeled, cored and chopped
125g Demerara sugar
100g butter
125ml double cream

Method:

1. Melt the butter and sugar in a pan. Add the pears and cook until golden. Allow to cool. (You can use the same pan for the sauce).
2. Beat the eggs lightly in a bowl.
3. Add the half the pears and half of the ginger and mix well.
4. Add the bicarbonate of soda, the flour and the breadcrumbs to the mixture.
5. Butter a large heat-resistant bowl and pour the syrup from the ginger into it. Arrange the rest of the pears and ginger over the syrup.
6. Pour the mixture into the bowl, cover with greaseproof paper and then foil, and leave to stand for 5 minutes.
7. Place the bowl in the top of a double boiler and steam for two hours.
8. To make the sauce, put the pears, the sugar and the butter into a heavy based pan and heat gently, stirring from time to time until the sugar has dissolved. Bring to the boil, add the cream and leave to cool.
9. Turn the pudding out onto a plate and pour the sauce over it.

Food producers
An A-Z list

Where to buy local products

An A-Z list

Best of British Organic Delicatessen
12 Broad Street, Bath, BA1 5LJ
www.bestofbritishdeli.co.uk
01225 448055
Opening hours:
Monday – Saturday: 9am – 5pm

Chandos Deli
12 George Street Bath, Avon, BA1 2EH
www.chandosdeli.com
01225 314 418
Opening hours:
Monday – Saturday: 9am – 5pm
Sunday: 11am – 5pm

Darling Deli
The Avenue, Combe Down, Bath,
BA2 5EH
www.darlingdeli.co.uk
 01225 835118
Opening hours:
Monday – Friday: 8.30am – 4pm
Saturday: 8.30am – 2pm

Dick Willows Farm and Cider shop
Box Road, Bathford, BA1 7LR
www.dickwillows.com
01225 859780
Opening hours:
Monday – Saturday: 9am – 6pm
Sunday: 11am – 5pm

Farrington's Farm Shop
Home Farm, Main Street, Farrington Gurney,
BS39 6UB
http://farringtons.co.uk
01761 452266
Opening hours:
Monday – Saturday: 8am – 7pm
Sunday 9am – 5pm

Fine Cheese Company
29-31 Walcot Street, Bath, BA1 5BN
www.finecheese.co.uk
01225 483407
Opening hours:
Monday – Friday: 9.30am – 5.30pm
Saturday: 9am – 5.30pm

Goodies Deli
2A St. Saviours Road, Larkhall, Bath,
BA1 6RT
www.goodiesdeli.co.uk
01225 336033
Opening hours:
Monday – Friday: 8am – 5pm
Saturday: 8.30am – 4pm

Hartley Farm Shop
202A Hartley, Winsley, Bradford-on-Avon,
BA15 2JB
www.hartley-farm.co.uk
01225 864948
Opening hours:
Monday – Saturday: 9am – 5.30pm
Sunday: 10am – 2.30pm

Harvest
37 Walcot Street, Bath, BA1 5BN
www.harvest-bath.coop
01225 465519
Opening hours:
Monday – Saturday: 9am – 6pm

Larkhall butcher, 1 Lambridge Buildings,
Bath, BA1 6RS
www.larkhallbutchers.co.uk
01225 313 987
Opening hours:
Monday – Friday: 6.30am – 5pm
Saturday: 6.30am – 1.30pm

Where to buy local products

(Continued)

Nibbles Cheese Shop
53 Guildhall Market, Green Park, Bath,
BA2 4AW
www.bathguildhallmarket.co.uk/nibbles-cheese-shop
01225 460213
Opening hours:
Monday – Friday: 8.30am – 5pm
Saturday: 8.30am – 5.30pm

Neston Park
Bath Road Atworth, Melksham, Wiltshire
SN12 8HP
www.nestonparkfarmshop.com
01225 700881
Opening hours:
Monday – Saturday: 9am – 5pm
Sunday: 10am – 4pm

Newton Farm Foods
Newton St Loe, Bath, BA2 9BT.
www.newtonfarmfoods.co.uk
01225 873707
Opening hours:
Monday – Saturday: 7am – 5.30pm
Sunday: 10am – 4pm

Paxton and Whitfield
1 John Street Bath, BA1 2JL
www.paxtonandwhitfield.co.uk
01225 466403
Opening hours:
Monday: 10am - 6pm
Tuesday – Saturday: 9.30am – 6pm

PJ's Farm Market Stall
Green Park Station, Bath, BA1 1JB
www.pjs-farm.co.uk
01179 324173
Opening hours:
All day Fridays and Saturdays

Prior Park Garden Centre
Prior Park Road, Bath, BA2 4NF
www.priorparkgardencentre.co.uk
01225 427175
Opening hours:
Monday – Friday: 8.30am – 6pm
Saturday: 10.30am – 4.30pm

Somerset Local Food
Roger White: www.localfooddirect.co.uk
Place orders by Tuesday for delivery on
Thursday or Friday.

Tasting Room
6 Green Street, Bath, BA1 2JY
www.tastingroom.co.uk
01225 483070
Opening hours:
Monday – Saturday: 9.30am – 6pm
Sunday: 10.30am – 5pm

The Tollshed
The Tollgate Inn, Ham Close, Holt,
BA14 6PX
www.tollgateholt.co.uk
01225 782326
Opening times:
Tuesday – Saturday: 9.30am – 5.30pm
Sunday: 10.30am – 3pm

Woody's Farm S hop
Farleigh Road, Norton St Phillip, Bath,
BA2 7NG
www.woodysfarmshop.co.uk
01225 720006
Opening hours:
Monday – Saturday: 9am – 5pm
Sunday: 10am – 5pm

Farmer's Markets

Some of the main farmers' markets in the area, and when they are held

Axbridge: Market Square	1st Saturday each month: 9am – 1pm
Bath: Green Park	Every Saturday: 9am – 1pm
Bradford on Avon: Westbury Gdns	3rd Thursday each month: 9am – 1.30pm
Chippenham: Market Place	Alternate Tuesdays: 9am – 1.30pm
Corsham: High Street	3rd Saturday each month: 9am – 1pm
Devizes: Market Place	1st Saturday each month: 9am – 1pm
Frome: Cheese and Grain	2nd Saturday each month: 9am – 1pm
Glastonbury: High Street	4th Sunday each month: 9am – 1pm
Keynsham: High Street	2nd Saturday each month: 9am – 1pm
Midsomer Norton: High Street	1st Saturday each month: 9am – 1pm
Swindon: Old Town	Last Friday each month: 9am – 1.30pm
Outlet Village	Every Sunday: 10am – 4pm
Trowbridge: Fore Street	4th Sunday each month: 9am – 1.30pm
Warminster: Central Car Park	1st and 3rd Friday each month: 9am – 12.30pm
Wells: Market Place	Every Wednesday: 9am – 2.30pm
Wootton Bassett: 4th Saturday each month:	9am – 1.30pm

Some useful websites:

www.afsl.org.uk/local_food: Local eating for global change: Action for sustainable living
www.bathfarmersmarket.co.uk
www.fresh-n-local.co.uk: Gloucestershire Farmers' Markets
www.makinglocalfoodwork.co.uk
www.rbst.org.uk: Rare breeds survival trust: 'conserving Britain's native farm livestock.'
ww.slowfood.org.uk
www.soilassociation.org
www.somersetfarmersmarkets.co.uk
www.sustainweb.org/eatsomerset
www.wiltshirefarmersmarkets.co.uk

Photograph provided by
Bath Farmers Market

Image provided by Bath Farmer's Market

Some of my favourite ingredients

Cheeses:
Obviously it is easy to find and use the excellent Cheddar cheeses in this area. However, it is more difficult to find equivalents of European cheeses that have been made locally. I have found a goat's cheese, which is comparable to Pecorino (a sheep's cheese) – Old Ford, made by Sleight Farm.
For a light cream cheese you can use Homewood 'fresh' ewe's cheese. Tim Homewood also makes excellent halloumi and marinated ewe's cheese (a feta-style cheese)

Cider vinegar:
I always use cider vinegar, made locally by KG consultants, available at Bath Farmers' Market. There are no additives, and it is not filtered, so retains its minerals and vitamins. It is also properly aged, so has had plenty of time to achieve a fully mature flavour.

Dairy:
My favourite milk is from Jersey or Guernsey cows. It is so creamy and delicious, and also contains fat-soluble vitamins that are not in skimmed milk. The cream is rich and wonderful – any other cream now tastes empty to me! I buy from Andy of Dreamers Farm at Bath Farmers' Market, but Hurdlebroodk Farm (Somerset) and Ivy House Farm (Beckington) also make very good products.

English pickled walnuts:
Despite the fact that we have plenty of walnut reees growing in this country, the only English Pickled walnuts I could find are in the Fine Cheese Company on Walcot Street, in Bath.

Horseradish sauce:
Strong horseradish cream: Tracklements, Wiltshire. www.tracklements.co.uk
Creamed horseradish sauce: Rose Farm, Wiltshire. www.rosefarmsomerset.co.uk

Jams, jellies and pickles
Angela's Kitchen products are lovely: you can find them at Bath Farmers' Market.

Mustard:
Tewkesbury mustard: Kitchen Garden, Stroud. www.kitchengardenpreserves.co.uk
Horseradish mustard (wholegrain): Tracklements. www.tracklements.co.uk

Oil:
I use extra virgin rapeseed oil because it is made locally and is excellent. It is better than olive oil as it is higher in omega 3, and has half the saturated fat. It has a high flashpoint so is good for cooking as well as for use in salads and dressings.

Index